MC
1650
N

The Third World and
the Rich Countries

Angelos Angelopoulos
translated by
N. Constantinidis
C. R. Corner
foreword by
Josué de Castro

The Praeger Special Studies program—
utilizing the most modern and efficient book
production techniques and a selective
worldwide distribution network—makes
available to the academic, government, and
business communities significant, timely
research in U.S. and international economic, social, and political development.

The Third World and the Rich Countries

Prospects for the Year 2000

Praeger Publishers   New York   Washington   London

PRAEGER SPECIAL STUDIES IN INTERNATIONAL ECONOMICS AND DEVELOPMENT

PRAEGER PUBLISHERS
111 Fourth Avenue, New York, N.Y. 10003, U.S.A.
5, Cromwell Place, London S.W.7, England

Published in the United States of America in 1972
by Praeger Publishers, Inc.

© 1972 by Praeger Publishers, Inc.

Library of Congress Catalog Card Number: 72-75694

Printed in the United States of America

Josué de Castro

Never before in history have human relation-
ships been as strained as they are today. Social
tensions between racial, political, and ideological
classes and groups, as well as between countries or
groups of countries, have reached a frightening in-
tensity and constitute a threat to world peace, to
the national security of peoples, and even to mankind's very survival. Never has there been so
critical a period in history as that in which we
are now living.

One of the most disturbing and indeed outra-
geous aspects of the present world crisis is the
disparity between the rates of growth of wealth in
two antagonistic groups of countries: the rich and
well-developed countries on the one hand and the
poor and underdeveloped countries on the other.
This disparity has created and is perpetuating the
world phenomenon of underdevelopment, which is
rightly regarded as the greatest scandal of our
century.

The gulf between the two groups is widening
continually. One no longer even talks of filling
it: that would be too utopian! The talk is rather
of throwing bridges across it. Everyone seems
agreed as to the failure of the development programs in the less developed regions. It has become
evident that the strategy employed was based on
principles and concepts that foredoomed it. Therefore, attempts are now being made to discover what
were the weaknesses that made the development

Josué de Castro is a professor at the Univer-
sité de Paris, President of the Centre International
pour le Développement, and former President of the
Council of the Food and Agricultural Organization.

planning a failure and what new development strategy would be capable of averting the grave dangers inherent in the growth disparity between the two coexisting but nonintegrated worlds--a disparity between development and plenty on the one hand and underdevelopment and poverty on the other.

As a result of the mistakes that have undoubtedly been made, the development efforts, taken as a whole, have not amounted to much. The most serious mistake was to assume that development planning today must of necessity be on the lines of the process of development that brought prosperity to countries of the Western world in the past.

A kind of "ethnocentrism" has led a majority of modern development theorists to base their ideas and their proposed systems on the concepts of the classical school of economists, who almost entirely failed to comprehend the problem of economic development in the dependent and backward regions of the world. These theorists ignore the fact that there is no such thing as an integrated world economy but only a Western economy full of contradictions, a socialist economy still in the stage of experiment and evolution, and a more or less primitive trading system in the rest of the world. Therefore, not much study has been devoted to the economic structures of this "rest of the world," a field that has been abandoned to the sociologists, or rather the "folklorists." One has tended to overlook the human beings who inhabit these regions, with their traditional cultures so far removed and different from Western forms of civilization. It had been thought that, by injections of capital and the introduction of inventions and technological innovations, it would be possible to change the general picture of traditional, non-Western structures and promote balanced development throughout the world. This miracle has not happened, and the result has been a widespread atmosphere of disillusionment and pessimism, and a fatalistic acceptance of the backwardness of the Third World as a virtually insoluble problem. That these countries are underdeveloped, the Western pessimists now say, is in the

nature of things; it is a consequence of biological
fatality or geographical determinism or natural conditions that exclude the possibility of real autonomous development.

These notions are of course utterly false.
The underdeveloped regions are kept in a permanently unfavorable economic situation by the "force of
circumstances," not by the "nature of things": by
the force of political or historical circumstances,
and in particular the political and economic colo-
nialism that has kept these regions outside the or-
bit of a world economy in rapid evolution. When
attempts are made to disguise the fact that the development problem is above all a political problem,
and that there are no cultural systems that are incapable of developing, one comes to doubt whether
certain highly developed and rich countries have
any real desire to help the poor and underdeveloped
countries out of the miserable condition in which
they at present exist. Is not "aid" in certain
cases a myth or, even worse, a deliberate misrepre-
sentation? Such then are some of the highly complex aspects of the problem of development that
call for study.

Numerous books have recently been written on
this subject, but few of their authors approach it
without prejudice and with an open mind.

In the present important work by Angelos
Angelopoulos, formerly a professor at the University of Athens and a well-known sociologist and
economist, the reader will find a series of answers
to all these vital questions, as well as concrete
and constructive proposals for the adoption of a
new development strategy that should make it possible to accelerate the economic and social progress of the Third World. By its well documented
reasoning, its penetrating analysis of the problem,
the originality of its proposals (particularly with
regard to development financing), and the new light
it throws on certain little understood aspects of
the mechanics of development, this work is of outstanding importance at the present juncture.

The author's remarks regarding the widening gulf between the rich and the poor countries, and the highly inequitable distribution of world income, are all the more convincing in that he is the first to have attempted to estimate gross world income, including that of the socialist countries, by using the Western method of computation.

While not underestimating the progress achieved by the developing countries in certain domains during the past twenty years, he emphasizes that the rates of growth reached by them during this period cannot be regarded as satisfactory, and among the causes of this inadequacy he stresses the ineffectualness of "development aid." He points out, _inter alia_, that of the annual sum of $12-14 billion that the international organizations regard as "development aid," only one-third--that is to say about $4 billion--might perhaps merit the description of "free aid." The rest is nothing more than a form of financing on unfavorable terms, resulting in the accumulation by the developing countries of a crushing burden of indebtedness. To show to what extent the so-called "gift element" is a euphemism, **Mr.** Angelopoulos points out that if this "gift" were in fact genuinely free assistance, and if poor countries were not obliged to pay high rates of interest, the external indebtedness of all the underdeveloped countries--less the amounts paid to date in respect of debt amortization--should not exceed $10 billion; whereas, in fact, according to the World Bank's figures, the external indebtedness of these countries amounted to $60 billion on January 1, 1970. That this enormous difference of $50 billion must appear inexplicable to the uninitiated is, according to the author, due to the fact that purely financing operations have been represented as being in the nature of "generous gifts."

Mr. Angelopoulos very rightly stresses the urgent necessity of adopting radical measures within the framework of a new development strategy, particularly in the matter of financing, which must be "priority number one." The easing of the burden of old debts, whose servicing already absorbs 65 percent

of new so-called aid capital, and the adoption of a
new financing system under which loans will be
granted to poor countries interest-free, are two
closely related measures without which a new "sisachty" (cancelling of debts) will become inevitable.

As regards the sources of financing, Mr.
Angelopoulos calculates that a genuinely free contribution by the industrialized countries equal to
0.5 percent of their GNP, in addition to a share
in the plus-value that would be created in the event
of a revaluation of gold, should be more than sufficient to cover the cost of the financing.

We now come to the second proposal that the
author put forward for the first time in a memorandum addressed to Robert S. McNamara, President of
the World Bank, in December, 1968, on the occasion
of the formation of the Pearson Commission. If for
various reasons the revaluation of gold were to become inevitable, the resultant plus-value should
most certainly not--for the reasons set forth by
the author--accrue in their entirety to the gold-
holding central banks. That plus-value must be regarded as "the patrimony of mankind as a whole,"
and a certain proportion of it must be devoted to
the financing of the poorer countries. My personal
opinion is that this proportion should not be one-
third, as Mr. Angelopoulos suggests, but one-half.
Only on this condition would a revaluation of gold
be regarded as equitable by public opinion. Assuming that the price of gold were raised either (1) by
30 percent or (2) by 70 percent (following the Roosevelt precedent), what possible justification could
there be for the developed countries profiting to
the extent of $12 billion in the first case or no
less than $28 billion in the second?

Many other complex (and in some cases hitherto
undiscussed) aspects of the problem are examined in
this book, which can thus serve as a valuable vade
mecum for those involved in the campaign against
underdevelopment. In our opinion, this campaign
cannot be successful unless it is accompanied by
certain radical--not to say revolutionary--

structural changes on a world scale. However, revolutionary changes cannot be suddenly improvised: they must be carefully planned in advance or they will come to naught. In the case of the "necessary revolution" that the world crisis imposes, it is essential to know exactly what is the nature of this crisis so that the "revolution" can be directed along the lines that will lead to the desired result. The present book makes a valuable contribution to the creation of the necessary "revolutionary" spirit without which the world will drift into ultimate catastrophe.

The peoples of the world must come to understand that they are all members of a single community and that only the active pursuit of a policy of international collaboration and solidarity can ensure universal peace and prosperity.

CONTENTS

LIST OF TABLES

LIST OF FIGURES

LIST OF ABBREVIATIONS

DAC	Development Assistance Committee
FAO	Food and Agriculture Organization of the United Nations
GATT	General Agreement on Tariffs and Trade
GDP	Gross Domestic Product
GMP	Gross Material Product
GNP	Gross National Product
IBRD	International Bank for Reconstruction and Development (World Bank)
IDA	International Development Association
ILO	International Labor Organization
IMF	International Monetary Fund
NMP	Net Material Product
NNP	Net National Product
OECD	Organization for Economic Cooperation and Development
UNCTAD	United National Conference on Trade and Development
UNDP	United National Development Program
UNIDO	United National Industrial Development Organization

The Third World and
the Rich Countries

INTRODUCTION: TOWARD A MORE JUST AND HUMANE WORLD

If we are really to understand the great problems of today, to discover their causes, and to foresee their effects on the economic and social structure of the world of tomorrow, we must awaken to the fact that we are living in a new period of history in which economic, social, political, and cultural conditions bear little resemblance to those that prevailed up to as recently as the end of World War I.

Mankind now finds itself at the opening stage of yet another great revolution. The most important factors that are determining the nature and course of this revolution are as follows:

1. <u>The immense advances that are being made in science and technology</u>. These developments, resulting from recent discoveries made, in particular, in the fields of nuclear energy and cybernetics, are destined to accelerate economic growth and social progress at an unprecedented rate, to bring about far-reaching changes in present economic, social, and political structures, and to lead finally to a unified social system on a world scale.

Man has now succeeded in taking off from our
planet, landing on the moon, and returning safely
to earth. He is now able to explore space with the
aid of mechanisms teleguided from earth. The in-
credible advances already made by science and technology, with those that will undoubtedly follow in
the years ahead, open up the brightest prospects
for the future of mankind.

2. The division of the world into two opposing sociopolitical systems. This dichotomy is a
standing threat to peace and an obstacle in the
path to world prosperity, but it is at the same
time a factor accelerating scientific and technological progress. It is a regrettable fact that
the scientific and technical revolution now in
progress would not yet have begun if its genesis
had not been precipitated by military exigencies
dictated by the race of the two opposing blocs for
supremacy. If the world had not been thus divided,
atomic power and computers would not have become
an integral part of industrial life so rapidly, and
space exploration and flights to the moon would
exist only in science fiction. Furthermore, the
fissures that are beginning to appear within the
two blocs, and the meteoric rise of the People's
Republic of China, complicate and intensify the
repercussions of this "plurality" of antagonistic
powers and will, in the end, result in profound
cleavages and radical changes in present structures,
both national and international.

3. The appearance of the new countries on the
international scene. These countries, which have
recently obtained independence and which form what
is called "the Third World," will in the long run
upset present states of equilibrium. Because of
their determination to catch up with the economically developed countries, and because of their population explosion, these new countries are destined
to ultimately play an outstanding role in world
evolution.

In the course of this study, we shall analyze
the great problems that face the countries of the

Third World, the difficulties with which they must contend, and their prospects in the world of tomorrow.

4. <u>Pressure by the workers and by the young generation</u>. The continuous and powerful pressure exerted by the workers, backed by young people, students, and intellectuals, with a view of securing a fairer distribution of the fruits of collective progress, reinforces the trend toward the creation of a more just and humane society. To achieve their aims, these dynamic elements of the population have no hesitation in seeking to overthrow outdated structures with a view to their replacement by new political and social systems better adapted to the needs of the society of their dreams. The workers do not limit their claims to immediate and material objectives but raise the whole question of the organization of society. They are critical of the structures of the capitalist and communist systems alike, and their attitude, together with the demonstrations by peasant farmers, shopkeepers, and artisans in various countries, adds up to an outright rejection of the present social system.

It is among the youth of today that discontent is most intense. Never has the gap between generations been as deep as it is today. Never have there been so many well-educated young people with little or no prospect of rising to executive status, and never has the executive age level been so high. Youth is thus in revolt against the injustice of a social system that excludes it from jobs that carry the power of decision-making. It is therefore understandable that the man of today refuses to be integrated in a system when he is not given the right to question its value and objectives.

What is certain is that these protests and demonstrations cannot be regarded as a mere passing phenomenon. As time goes on, they will become more violent and their impact increasingly greater. This is only too obvious if one reflects that at

the present time the growing proportion of young
people under 25 has already reached 55 percent of
total population and that with the generalization
of education there will be an ever-increasing demand by the new generations, born and educated in
a world seething with revolutionary ideas, to be
admitted to a more active participation in economic
and political life.

5. The rational utilization of world resources. With a view to attaining higher rates of
economic growth and improved standards of living,
great changes are being made in the administration
and management of enterprises, which are becoming
gigantic and multinational, and this makes a reorientation of economic and social policy imperative.

Here the social sciences have a highly important contribution to make. In particular, the modern science of economics, which has "mathematized"
itself by the adoption of econometric models and
"humanized" itself by the study of social objectives, is enormously assisting the rational administration of national and international resources.
Thus, the science of economics, which during most
of the nineteenth century found itself primarily in
the service of the countries of Europe that were
embarking at that time on the process of industrialization, from about 1930 onward began to adjust
itself to the new conditions and to modernize itself so as to serve in particular--but this time in
a conscious and deliberate manner--countries in the
process of development, which were seeking the most
efficient way of overcoming their immense backwardness as compared with the industrialized countries.
Faced with this new situation, the economists were
obliged to rethink the classical postulates to permit the revision of existing economic policy in the
light of the new social orientation.

All these factors have generated the driving
forces that give the present age its revolutionary
aspect, the essence of which is the demand for the
creation of a world that shall be better, more just,

more humane. Furthermore, recent technical and
scientific progress has been so formidable that, if
the risk of a new and cataclysmic world war is to
be eliminated, the establishment of the interdependence of, and peaceful coexistence between, all
peoples must be the supreme aim.

This new situation must have as corollary a
new way of thinking. And one of the problems that
demands new thinking is the fact that, so long as
the populations of some countries remain in a state
of "chronic famine," social disorders and civil
wars will continue to gangrene the greater part of
the world and the revolutionary elements everywhere
will continue to exercise their virulent activity.

In the future, the risk of world war could lie
in the immense and still widening gap between the
rich and the poor countries. If the risk of such a
conflict is to be averted, there must be a radical
and urgent revision of the policy that has prevailed over the last twenty years, a policy that
has not only failed to produce satisfactory results
but that, on the contrary, has brought the developing countries to an impasse from which escape seems
almost impossible.

The object of the ideas we shall put forward
in the following pages is solely to assist in the
search for concrete and effective ways of helping
these countries to overcome the immense difficulties with which they are grappling and to acquire
a real prospect of future prosperity.

What we would like to stress here and now is
that nothing can prevent the economic and social
development of the countries of the Third World.
The countries that are now poor will succeed in
achieving prosperity in much less time than the now
developed countries took to do so. Thanks to the
immense technological progress made in the already
developed countries, the industrialization of the
young nations will be achieved sooner or later in
new and unprecedented conditions, even if the rich

countries were to reduce or suspend their aid. To
think otherwise would be mistaken and dangerous.
The only result of an unhelpful attitude on the
part of the rich countries would be to create a
hostile climate that could only end in bloody conflict. The immense changes in the size of the populations of the countries of the Third World, which
by the end of the present century will account for
three-quarters of total world population, may eventually change the whole aspect of the geopolitical
map of the world thanks to the technical equipment
that science and technology are making available to
them.

If the nineteenth century was the era of Great
Britain and Europe and the twentieth century is
that of the United States and the Soviet Union, the
twenty-first century may well be that of Asia and
Africa.

THE MEASUREMENT OF ECONOMIC DEVELOPMENT

Out of a total of 132 member-countries of the
United Nations, more than 100 are classified as
"underdeveloped" or, to use the term adopted by the
international agencies, "developing" countries.
This group of countries has come to be known as the
"Third World."*

Which are these developing countries? By what
criteria are we to distinguish between developing
and developed countries? Does economic and social
development lend itself to quantitative measurement?

---

*This term was coined in 1952 by Alfred Sauvy
at the height of the cold war and applied to the
nonaligned developing countries that remained outside the two power blocs but belonged to the non-
communist world. As explained subsequently, the
concept of the "Third World" is used here in a
broader and more specific sense.

Three Indicators of Development

The definition of underdevelopment has been the subject of long controversy. A series of special studies undertaken by the Department of Economic and Social Affairs of the United Nations Secretariat on the feasibility of measuring economic progress has not yielded satisfactory results. The definition formerly adopted, namely that a developing country is marked by a "suboptimal utilization of its available material and human resources," can no longer serve as a meaningful criterion for it is not possible on the one hand to scientifically define "optimal utilization" or on the other hand to adopt a method of diagnosis of underdevelopment that would permit a valid distinction between developing and developed nations. Moreover, the extreme diversity of the degrees of underdevelopment or backwardness precludes any simple classification of countries or regions according to geographical location, e.g., countries in Asia, in Africa, in the Far East, in Latin America, and so on. In other words, the classification cannot be made merely on the basis of regional diversification or homogeneity.

Economic development is in fact a highly complex phenomenon, and some of its determinant factors do not readily lend themselves to quantitative measurement. According to a recent study by the United Nations, an appraisal of the state of development of a given country and its progress over a specific period of time requires the evaluation of performance in three separate spheres, namely: (1) the production of goods and services, (2) the level of living of the inhabitants, and (3) the changes in the capacity of the economy to deliver needed goods and services in the future.[1]

Hence, in studying the various aspects of the process of development it is no longer sufficient to consider exclusively those relating to the production of goods and services. It is equally important to take into account the decision and

policy-making mechanisms of the modern state and
its various agencies, whose function is to assist
individuals in raising the future productive capacity of the economy and thereby achieving their numerous objectives. (Development is thus a dynamic
process involving a series of continuous changes
that are the end product of efforts designed to
raise the level of productivity of the economy and
ultimately improve the living standard of the population.)

The Social Character of Development

The modern concept of economic growth lays
special emphasis on the necessity for social development.[2] It is nowadays realized that the targets
of accelerated economic growth cannot be achieved
within the framework of a static or rigid political
and social structure. Moreover, the formulation of
the major objectives of development becomes impossible within a rigid social order and a short time
horizon. A major prerequisite for rapid development acceptable to all is the application of policy
measures designed to effect a radical transformation
of the existing socioeconomic structure and improvements in social conditions. (Developing countries
are compelled to introduce a series of reforms as
regards land tenure, tax structure, income distribution, employment policy, public health, and education. Last but not least, development requires the
creation of conditions permitting effective participation by the people in the mechanism of political
and economic power.) The aforesaid policy measures
are desirable not only from the point of view of
social justice and political equality but also as
directly conducive to the greater efficiency of the
whole process of development.(Moreover, they constitute the instruments of a development program
capable of stimulating the will and increasing the
ability of the people to make a sustained effort to
achieve higher levels of progress.)

A socially oriented development effort is
equally indispensable for the abolition of

obstacles, both structural and institutional, that
tend to inhibit growth. Among the major impedi-
ments to growth are the excessive concentration of
wealth and income, the system under which the more
well-to-do families own the basic factors of production, and the traditional attitude of opposition
to change and innovation.

It would be erroneous, as is rightly under-
lined in the Tinbergen Report, to assert that the
lessening of inequalities in income and wealth and
the acceleration of economic growth are necessarily
conflicting aims.[3] According to this report,
studies undertaken in developing countries have
confirmed that farms operated under a regime of
large landowners have a lower level of productivity,
while the concentration of economic power in industry and finance stifles competition, impedes development, and is often used in the pursuit of objectives incompatible with development. In this respect, agrarian reform in the developing countries
is of supreme priority, especially in view of the
sustained rapid growth of the agricultural population.

Therefore, it should be obvious that the modern development process, with special emphasis on
social development, must achieve the fusion of economic and social aims into a single overriding objective. (Development should no longer be regarded
exclusively as the raising of the level of production of goods and services: it must comprise profound transformation of the social structure and,
above all, of the system of distribution of national
income, thereby improving the living standard of
the masses.) (In this context, an increase in national income is only one of the indicators of development. In the full sense of the term, development must comprise a broadening of the opportunities for all social classes to secure a better
life and the elimination of all hindrances and all
injustices that impede the modernization of the social structure.[4] One should never forget that the
pattern of human behavior is a dominant factor in
the process of development and that the dream of

equality has fired people's imagination and urged
them to cooperate constructively in the fulfillment
of increasingly ambitious tasks. Should the ruling
classes in the developing countries fail to satisfy
the aspirations of their peoples, and especially of
youth, the existing social structure will inexora-
bly be overthrown by force.[5]

Only through such a global development strat-
egy--both on the national and the international
level--can there be any hope of achieving one of
the crucial objectives of our time, namely, to provide gainful employment for the huge reserves of
employable manpower. The magnitude of the task
ahead can be judged by the fact that over the decade 1970-80 the world's employable population is
expected to increase by 280 million, of which as
many as 226 million will swell the labor potential
of the developing countries where large-scale unemployment and underemployment are of chronic character. Here is a problem that there is no hope of
solving unless it is regarded and dealt with as a
world problem.

The Validity of GNP as a
Criterion of Development

Although it may be possible to measure, for
individual countries, the state of socioeconomic
performance (per capita GNP, standards of nutrition,
infant mortality, life expectancy, monetary and
price stability, levels of savings, unemployment
and underemployment), it is far from easy to assess
on a world scale the dynamic aspects of development
and to determine the indicators of the future economic potential. To make an international comparison of national indicators of socioeconomic performance is a most difficult task since it encounters conceptual and statistical obstacles that tend
to distort the resulting observations and lead to
erroneous conclusions.

Of the three indicators of socioeconomic performance mentioned earlier, that of total production
of goods and services, or GNP, is accepted as the

most reliable for international comparisons of levels of development.* Moreover, it can serve as a useful aid in distinguishing developed from developing countries. However, the international comparison of per capita GNP should not be taken as a precise measure of the state of development of each country. It is not a satisfactory indicator of a country's socioeconomic performance since it excludes determinants of prime importance in the process of development, such as economic structures, social and cultural factors, the system of income distribution, and the mechanism of social and economic decision-making by the central authorities, all of which have a direct impact on a country's future productive capacity. Moreover, the concept of GNP is subject to controversy and is often a misleading yardstick since it contains an aggregation of both "positive" and "negative" elements without all of them representing components of human welfare. Thus, the cost of administration must be added to the outlay on the production of goods and services, so that an increase in the number of civil servants and other government employees automatically raises the GNP without a corresponding rise in real terms. Furthermore, the inadequacy of the available statistical data, the frequent disparities between official rates of exchange and the real purchasing power of the relative national currencies, the divergent trends in domestic and world price levels, the different methods of computation which vary according to the social and political

----

*According to the concepts and definitions adopted by world specialized agencies, GNP at market prices measures the value of all the goods and services produced within the country during a year before deduction of depreciation charges and other allowances for business and institutional consumption of durable capital goods. National income equals GNP less depreciation charges, indirect taxes, and subsidies. For a more detailed analysis of the concept of income, see the Appendix.

regime of the country, and the lack of unanimity as
to the concept of GNP and its components are all
factors that render international comparisons du-
bious and often quite misleading.

Despite these reservations, the GNP should for
practical purposes be accepted as a reasonable
yardstick for the quantitative appraisal of inter-
temporal changes, as a distinguishing line between
developed and developing nations, and as a basis
for international comparisons of levels of development. (This method is being adopted by the Department of Economic and Social Affairs of the United
Nations, the World Bank, and other international
agencies.)

Again, the level of GNP ultimately determines
the living standard of the population by retarding
or accelerating the rate of socioeconomic progress.
If the total production of goods and services remains low, a country cannot hope to provide its inhabitants with a better standard of living since
there can be no growth in the productive capacity
of the economy. This is the typical case of a developing country caught in a situation of self-
perpetuating stagnation.)

THE VICIOUS CIRCLE OF POVERTY

In practice, a low income level is both the
cause and the effect of certain characteristics
common to almost all developing countries. The
most important of these characteristics are as follows:

1. A high proportion of the working population
employed in agriculture using primitive farming
techniques,

2. Chronic nutritional deficiency in large
sections of the population,

3. Chronic unemployment and underemployment,

4. High rates of population growth,

5. Deficient infrastructure and inefficient industrialization,

6. Low level of scientific and technological know-how,

7. Low savings and investment levels and limited accumulation of capital,

8. Underutilization of natural resources,

9. Structural imbalances and economic dualism, i.e., the coexistence of modern and primitive economic sectors,

10. Excessive dependence on foreign trade and capital inflow,

11. Low income and living levels.

All these salient characteristics represent both structural imbalances and obstacles to economic development. They keep the utilization of the available material and human resources well below the potential optimum level. They tend to impede the formation and efficient use of capital and to retard improvements in technology and education. Moreover, the negative factors of the process of production create imbalances and rigidities that, if aggravated by an undue dependence on the outside world, culminate in one of the worst features of economic backwardness, namely, the vicious circle of poverty.[6] In fact, an economically retarded country is marked by low productivity and generally by a living standard so low as to leave little margin for saving and the formation of productive capital. Furthermore, the prevailing low incomes cannot maintain the level of demand required to boost production, while the shortage of savings accounts for the lack of profitable investment opportunities. Again, the utilization of material resources depends on the quantity and quality of the available labor force. Here the continuing high degree of illiteracy, the shortage of skilled labor, and the deficiencies in scientific and technological knowledge combine to form a serious barrier to economic development and tend both to aggravate and to perpetuate the vicious circle of poverty.

Within the context of this circular causation, the interaction of obstacles to growth and structural imbalances, as accentuated by widespread market imperfection, sets in motion a cumulative process that reinforces the general state of self-perpetuating social and economic stagnation.

Modern economics has adopted this cumulative circular process as an explanation of the fact that a poor country tends to remain poor because it is poor. However, such a situation of persistent economic backwardness is accentuated by the policies of the industrialized countries as regards international trade and aid. Far from helping the developing countries, by means of effective trade and aid policies, to break out of the vicious circle, the rich countries impose a system of economic domination. They are primarily interested in extracting maximum profits, with utter disregard for the aspiration of the poor countries to achieve balanced and rapid progress. The dependence of developing countries on the outside world is accentuated by the high degree of commodity and/or geographical concentration of their exports. Any deterioration in their terms of trade has serious repercussions on the foreign exchange earning capacity of the primary producing countries. Herein lies the impact of the so-called "international framework of development," which is determined by the conditions prevailing in the importing countries and the trends in the world markets. Thus, the mechanism of development tends to operate under conditions of self-perpetuating stagnation imposed on developing countries by the advanced market economies through their foreign trade policies.

All low-income countries with inadequate standards of living have a very limited capacity for capital accumulation and a highly unstable sector

of primary production. They fall within the large
group of less developed or developing nations often
referred to as the Third World.

Definition of Underdevelopment

Although for practical purposes GNP might perhaps serve as a rough dividing line between developed and developing countries, the problem presents
itself as to what is the level of per capita GNP
below which a country is to be classified as a developing country.

The Commission on International Development
under the chairmanship of Lester B. Pearson, which
made an extensive study of the problems of the
Third World, adopted national income as the criterion for distinguishing between developed and less
developed nations, and put the line of demarcation
at a level of $500 per capita per annum.[7] As no
other criterion is completely satisfactory since
there are some borderline cases of countries that
cannot be readily classified, we have taken the
$500 per capita annual income as a working yard-
stick. An additional reason for the choice lies in
the fact that the International Bank for Reconstruction and Development (IBRD) also has adopted the
$500 level. Moreover, any attempt to devise an al-
ternative measurement of economic development would
involve lengthy and confusing discussion.

Despite the acceptance of the above criterion
for the classification of developing countries, it
is considered advisable to extend the yardstick of
less than $500 per capita per year to all countries,
irrespective of their socioeconomic system. This
would permit the inclusion of such centrally
planned economies as the People's Republic of China,
North Korea, North Vietnam, Cuba, and others.
These are the developing countries of the communist
world. Thus, within this broader definition of
economic backwardness, the Third World would include both the developing countries of the market-
type economy and those of the centrally planned

system.   The distribution of world population in
1970 according to the threefold classification is
shown in Table 1.

According to Table 1, the group of developing
countries, or the Third World, accounts for as much
as 70 percent of total world population.   The remaining 30 percent is divided among developed market economies (20 percent) and developed centrally
planned economies (10 percent).

Regardless of the stage of development, about
68 percent of the population of the globe lives in
the market economy or capitalist countries, and
about 32 percent in the centrally planned or communist countries.

TABLE 1

Distribution of World Population, 1970

Group of Countries	Population (millions)	Percentage (approximate)
Developed market economies	715	20
Centrally planned economies	346	10
Developing countries (irrespective of social system)	2,523	70
Total	3,584	100

Source: United Nations, Demographic Yearbook,
1970 (New York, 1971).

DISTRIBUTION OF WORLD GNP IN 1970

An objective appraisal of the social and economic situation existing in the group of developing
nations, and an understanding of the nature and
magnitude of their main problems, requires an estimate of world income and its distribution among regions, countries, and social systems. As far as we
are aware, no attempt has been made to arrive at an
estimate of world income by either the various international agencies or any other specialized institutions.[8]

The United Nations Statistical Office pub-
lishes data on the national income of the market
economy countries and draws international comparisons of GDP and per capita GDP levels. Quite recently the same department made estimates of the
GNP of the centrally planned economies, without at-
tempting a comparison between the two groups of
countries since the method of calculating national
income differs. For this important reason, the
subject of enquiry of the Pearson Commission is
limited to the gross domestic income of the non-
communist world.

However, since the centrally planned economies
comprise almost one-third of the world's population,
it is essential to include their GNP in the computation of the world total.

The attempt to arrive at a uniform estimate of
the world GDP encounters certain methodological
difficulties. These are directly associated with
the Soviet concept of GNP as adopted by all the
centrally planned economies. According to this
concept, GNP is defined in a narrower sense, as
compared with the Western concept, in that it excludes all income generated by the sector of ter-
tiary production or the service sector of the economy. By contrast, in the market economies the contribution of the service sector to the formation of
the GNP is of prime importance.

Despite these methodological differences, we
shall attempt to estimate world GNP for the year

1970. The computation has been made on the basis
of three major sets of figures:

1. The developed market economies. The estimates of the Organization for Economic Cooperation
and Development (OECD) for 1969 have been adjusted
for 1970 according to the growth rate registered in
that year.

2. The developing market economies. In the
calculation of the GDP of the non-communist developing countries for 1970, use has been made of the
United Nations figures for 1967 adjusted by the 6
percent average annual rate of growth attained in
1968 and 1969.

3. The centrally planned economies. The Appendix gives an account of the method applied in
expressing the gross material product of the communist countries in terms of the western concept of
GNP. The calculations have been verified on the
basis of U.N. estimates, and it is hoped that the
computations (now attempted for the first time)
give a fair approximation to reality.

The results of the calculations of world GNP
are given in Table 2.

The figures in that table show (1) that while
the developing countries, both market economies and
centrally planned economies, account for as much as
69 percent of world population, they produce only
15.4 percent of world GNP and (2) that the developed
countries, with only 31 percent of world population,
account for no less than 84.6 percent of world GNP.
These broad aggregates clearly show the alarming
nature of the issues involved in the state of economic backwardness of so great a part of the world.

Table 3 shows the distribution of world GNP by
groups of countries classified according to their
socioeconomic system.

The figures in Table 3 show that the market
economies, both developed and developing, account
for approximately 68 percent of world population

TABLE 2

Distribution of World GNP and Population, 1970

	Population		GNP	
	Millions	Percentage	Billions	Percentage
DEVELOPED COUNTRIES				
Market economies				
United States	205	6.0	978	31.8
Canada	21	0.6	76	2.4
Western Europe	358	10.0	723	23.6
Japan	103	3.0	188	6.2
Other countries*	58	1.0	60	1.9
Total	745	20.6	2,025	65.9
Centrally planned economies				
U.S.S.R.	242	7.0	425	13.8
Eastern Europe	128	3.4	150	4.9
Total	370	10.4	575	18.7
Total (developed countries)	1,115	31.0	2,600	84.6
DEVELOPING COUNTRIES				
Market economies				
Asia, Africa, and Latin America	1,664	46.7	335	10.9
Centrally planned economies				
People's Republic of China	760	21.0	125	4.1
Other countries	45	1.3	12	0.4
Total	805	22.3	137	4.5
Total (developing countries)	2,489	69.0	472	15.4
WORLD TOTAL	3,584	100.0	3,072	100.0

*Australia, South Africa, New Zealand, and Israel.

TABLE 3

Distribution of World Population and GNP by Socioeconomic System, 1970

| Group of Countries | Population | | GNP | |
	Millions	Percentage	Billions of U.S. Dollars	Percentage
Market economy countries				
Developed	687	19	1,964	66
Developing	1,746	49	330	11
Total	2,433	68	2,294	77
Centrally planned economies				
Developed	346	10	563	19
Developing	805	22	137	4
Total	1,151	32	700	23
World Total	3,584	100	2,994	100

and 77 percent of world GNP, while the centrally
planned economies account for 32 percent of world
population and only 23 percent of world GNP.

The disparities are even more striking in the
distribution of world GNP within each major group of
countries, and in particular within the market economy or capitalist group. Thus, the market economies
of Western Europe, North America, Japan, and certain
other developed countries account for 39 percent of
the population and yet produce as much as 85.2 percent of the aggregate GNP of all market economies.
By contrast, the developing nations of this group
account for about 61 percent of the population and
only 14.2 percent of the combined GNP.[9] The United
States alone, with only 8.5 percent of the total
population of the market economies, produces no less
than 44 percent of the total GNP of the non-communist
world and 53 percent of that of the industrially advanced countries of the West.

The significance of the immense disparity in
the distribution of world GNP can be fully understood when it is noted that the per capita income
of $4,800 in the United States in 1970 was 45 times
greater than that of India. An income inequality
of such dimensions becomes even more striking when
one examines the distribution of the GNP within
each country of the non-communist world.

The group of centrally planned economies shows
similar income inequalities. The developed communist countries, with about 30 percent of the group's
total population, account for 80.5 percent of its total GNP as against 19.5 percent for the developing
communist countries. Of course, within the communist
countries the distribution of income per capita is
not marked by such wide disparities as in the market
economies. This more egalitarian distribution of
income is attributable to the nationalization of the
means of production, with labor and not capital as
the prime source of income. It is significant that
the U.S.S.R., with 20 percent of the population,
contributes no less than 60 percent of the aggregate
GDP of the communist countries and 75 percent of aggregate GDP in the developed communist countries.

Figures 1 and 2 illustrate the distribution of world GNP according to both the socioeconomic system and the stage of development of the countries.

The preceding figures clearly reveal widespread poverty all over the world. A very large section of humanity lives today in conditions of abject misery and below the "threshold of poverty."[10]

With the demarcation line between developed and developing countries fixed around a $500 per capita income per year, there are numerous nations with a much lower per capita income, as shown in Table 4. Inclusive of the communist countries in Asia, a total of almost two billion inhabitants have a per capita GNP of less than $200.

Malnutrition and Undernourishment

Whereas during the periods of great famine in the history of mankind millions of individuals were exterminated outright by hunger, nowadays millions of people are condemned to a lingering death over the coming decades through widespread nutritional deficiencies and the resulting low resistance to diseases.

The lack of basic nutrients for the maintenance of human health causes premature deaths and, under certain conditions, even impairs the mental faculties of the person suffering from a deficient intake of food. The world is therefore faced with the problem of "collective hunger," or with what Josué de Castro calls the "occult hunger" that affects in an endemic or epidemic form great masses of human beings. Owing to the lack of certain nutrients essential to human life, these masses are condemned to a slow death from starvation, "even though they may be eating daily."[11] It is estimated that about 30-50 percent of the world's population suffers from malnutrition, namely from food deficiency in terms of quality of food intake and about 10-15 percent from undernourishment in terms of quantities consumed. According to estimates of the Food and Agriculture Organization (FAO), the daily per capita intake of protein of animal origin

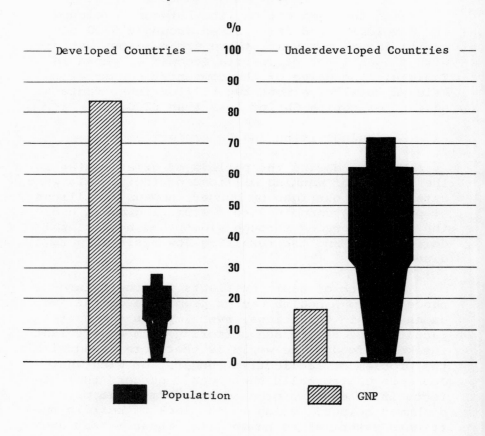

FIGURE 1

Population and GNP, 1970

FIGURE 2

Distribution of GNP by Social System, 1970

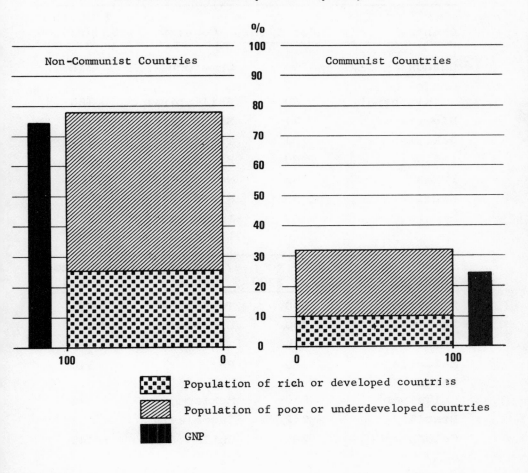

°/o

Non-Communist Countries

Communist Countries

100

Population of rich or developed countries

Population of poor or underdeveloped countries

GNP

TABLE 4

Classification of Developing Countries
by Per Capita GNP, 1968
(in 1964 U.S. dollars)

Country	Under $100	Country	$100 to Under $200
Uganda	94	Cameroon	118
Congo (Kinshasa)	80	Philippines	160
Nigeria	71	South Korea	160
Pakistan	91	Thailand	130
India	89	Bolivia	135
Burma	65	Morocco	190
Haiti	68	U.A.R.	157
		Indonesia	100

Country	$200 to Under $300	Country	$300 to Under $500
Algeria	200	Turkey	281
Zambia	200	Liberia	285
Guinea	215	Tunisia	285
Malaysia	283	Peru	310
China (Taiwan)	250	Mexico	476
Brazil	242	Yugoslavia	453
Colombia	281	Chile	445

Source: World Bank, Trends in Developing Countries (Washington, D.C., 1970), Tables 2, 4.

is 66 grams in North America and only 8 grams in
the Far East. Moreover, in almost all African
countries, the rate of infant mortality is five
times higher than in the developed nations. A conservative estimate puts the number of children who
die daily from hunger at about 10,000.

During the session of the United Nations International Children's Emergency Fund (UNICEF) in
Geneva in April, 1971, held to celebrate the
twenty-fifth anniversary of UNICEF's founding, it
was revealed that 50 percent of the children and
adults in the developing countries suffer from malnutrition and that their number will exceed the one
billion mark by 1980. This widespread malnutrition
has serious effects on the formation of the human
brain since, according to expert opinion, it should
attain 90 percent of its normal development during
the first five years of life. Furthermore, one-
third of the population of the developing nations
lives under primitive housing conditions in slums
and overcrowded towns.

Illiteracy is an equally widespread symptom of
underdevelopment. At present there are about 800
million illiterate people, or over 100 million more
than twenty years ago. Furthermore, the developing
countries with one doctor per 10,000 inhabitants
are a rare exception, whereas in the developed
countries there is one doctor for 750 inhabitants.

Nevertheless, it cannot be denied that public
health conditions in the developing countries have
improved significantly over the past two decades.
This is reflected in the increase in average life
expectancy from 30 to 50 years.

Striking Inequalities

The extent of prevailing poverty becomes even
more striking when one considers the inequality
in the distribution of national income in the

developing countries. Thus, a United Nations study
for Latin America reveals that 5 percent of the
population took no less than 31.5 percent of the
aggregate GNP, whereas the poorest class, representing 20 percent of the population, took only 3.5
percent of the GNP. Table 5 shows the share of the
GNP accruing to the privileged classes of the Latin
American countries.

From the data in Table 5, it is possible to
discern a uniform trend in the distribution of GNP
in all Latin American developing countries. Thus,
the upper 10 percent of the population takes no
less than 40-45 percent of the GNP; the upper 5
percent takes 30-35 percent; while almost 15 percent goes to the uppermost tiny minority of 1
percent. Moreover, according to a statement by
Robert S. McNamara, 75 percent of the land in
Brazil is owned by less than 10 percent of the total number of families.

The situation is even more deplorable in the
developing countries of Africa and Asia. A survey
of ten African developing countries has revealed an
excessive degree of concentration of wealth. For
instance, the wealthiest class comprising only 5
percent of the population receives no less than
40-50 percent of the GDP. The corresponding share
for the Congo (Kinshasa) amounts to 50 percent,
for Gabon to 47 percent, and for the Malagasy Republic to 39 percent. Again, similar evidence of
concentration of wealth can be found in four Asian
developing countries (India, Pakistan, Ceylon, and
the Philippines). In the Philippines, for instance, the poorest classes accounted for 17 percent of the total number of families (households)
in 1961 and for 3.3 percent of the GDP, whereas in
the top income bracket 1.4 percent of the households shared no less than 15.3 percent of the GDP.
In India, according to the estimates of the National Council for Research in Applied Economics, the
upper 10 percent of the population absorbed in 1960
as much as 36 percent of the GDP, while 12 percent
of the farming households owned over half the arable

TABLE 5

Indicators of Income Inequalities in Latin America

| Country | Year | Population | Share of Income | | |
			Upper 10 Percent	Upper 5 Percent	Top 1 Percent
Argentina	1961	Individuals	40.9	31.2	16.3
Brazil	1960	Individuals	45.0	33.0	18.0
Colombia	1962	Active Population	42.7	30.4	10.0
El Salvador	1961	Active Population	45.6	33.0	18.0
Venezuela	1962	Households	40.7	26.5	9.0
Panama	1960	Active Population	40.0	34.5	16.5
Mexico	1963	Households	41.5	29.0	12.0
Costa Rica	1961	Households	46.0	35.0	16.0

Source: Economic Survey of Latin America (New York: United Nations, 1969), Part 1.

land. According to an optimistic assumption of an
average annual growth rate of 3 percent for net per
capita income, it would take 30 years, until the
year 2000, for one-third of the households in India
to acquire a level of food consumption acceptable
by nutritional standards.[12] According to a different study sponsored by the Ford Foundation, about
40 percent of the rural population and 50 percent
of the urban population, or the equivalent of 22
million inhabitants, have failed to secure the minimum standard at which the intake of food can begin
to be considered acceptable. The present rates of
economic growth are inadequate to improve the extremely low levels of living. As the Ford Foundation study points out, thus far the benefits of
economic growth have gone to the rich sections of
the population. By contrast, the impoverished
masses experienced a lowering of their living standard during the 1960's.[13]

     There can be no doubt whatsoever that the de-
veloping countries in Asia, Africa, and Latin America are predominately poverty-stricken regions.
Moreover, persistent unemployment and underemployment is as high as 20 percent of the labor force.

THE PERSISTENT WIDENING OF THE GAP

     As time goes on, the problem of underdevelop-
ment assumes alarming proportions since, contrary
to all hopes, the gap between rich and poor nations
continues to widen instead of narrowing. On the
basis of experience acquired over the past two
decades, the outlook for the next ten-year period
is one of gloom since the existing gap is expected
to widen still further if the situation is allowed
to continue along the same lines.

     A simple calculation suffices to explain the
irresistible trend toward a broader gap between developed and developing nations. Given an average
annual rate of growth of 5 percent, which actually
represents the average growth for almost all the

countries of the world, the increase in the GNP per
capita per annum in the rich countries will be of
the order of $150, as against a mere $10 rise in
the developing countries. Furthermore, it has been
estimated that it will take 80 years for the developing countries to reach the present per capita income level of Western Europe. However, in the case
of the lowest-income developing countries, which
account for almost half the population of the whole
group of developing nations, the required period of
sustained effort will extend to 200 years.[14] The
present situation is both deplorable and absurd.

Developments over the Years 1950-70

According to the Pearson Report, aggregate
production of goods and services (GDP) over the period 1950-67 rose by an average annual rate of 4.8
percent for all developing countries of the non-
communist world.[15] The provisional figures indicate
the achievement of a similar growth rate for 1968
and 1969, and hence a 4.8 percent increase can
reasonably be assumed for the entire period 1950-69.
However, the whole picture undergoes a significant
change in the sense that an average 2.4 percent annual growth in population reduces the average annual real growth rate in the per capita GDP to 2.4
percent.

Over the period under consideration, the average annual growth rate of the GDP in the advanced
market economies was 4.3 percent while the per
capita GDP rose 3.1 percent annually as a result of
a slower rate of population growth. The relevant
figures are shown in Table 6.

According to the differential growth rates in
the GDP per capita per year, the rich countries attained an almost 46 percent faster rate of economic
growth than the developing nations, thereby contributing to the further widening, year after year,
of the already immense gap between the two groups
of countries. In order to form a better understanding of this process of inevitable widening, one

TABLE 6

Growth of GDP at Constant Prices, Population,
and Per Capita GDP, 1950-67
(Percentage per annum)

	Developing Countries	Industrialized Countries
GDP	4.8	4.3
Population	2.4	1.2
Per capita GDP	2.4	3.1

Source: Partners in Development: Report of
the Commission on International Development (New
York: Praeger Publishers, 1969), Table 3-1 and
Annex II, "Statistical Materials," Table 1.

should recall that the growth rates registered in
the advanced market economies relate to levels of
GDP much higher than those reached in the developing countries.

The rates of growth are even lower in the case
of developing nations which have been unable to
achieve the average annual rate of development of
4.8 percent and have a per capita GDP of less than
$150 per year. This is particularly true of sever-
al countries in Africa, Asia, and Latin America,
where the average annual growth rates are well below the general 4.8 percent.

The figures on the regional growth of GDP,
population, and GDP per capita per year at constant
prices (percent per year) for the years 1950-67 are
shown in Table 7.

It is clear from these estimates that in the
regions of Africa, Asia, and Latin America the GDP
per capita per year rose at an average annual rate
of 1.7 percent over the period 1950-67 as against
an overall 2.4 percent for the entire group of developing countries.

TABLE 7

Growth of GDP at Constant Prices, Population,
and Per Capita GDP, by Region, 1950-67
(percent per annum)

Region	1950-67 Growth
Africa	
GDP	4.0
Population	2.3
GDP per capita	1.7
South Asia	
GDP	3.8
Population	2.1
GDP per capita	1.7
East Asia	
GDP	5.1
Population	2.6
GDP per capita	2.4
Southern Europe	
GDP	6.0
Population	1.4
GDP per capita	4.5
Latin America	
GDP	4.8
Population	2.9
GDP per capita	1.8
Middle East	
GDP	6.5
Population	3.0
GDP per capita	3.4

Source: Partners in Development: Report of
the Commission on International Development (New
York: Praeger Publishers, 1969), Annex II, "Statistical Materials," Table 1.

Economic Growth in the Advanced
Market Economies

According to OECD, the rate of economic growth
in industrial countries in the last 25 years has
been substantially faster than in any earlier period of similar duration in recorded economic history.
Moreover, that faster growth is not a temporary or
accidental phenomenon but the result of governments
explicitly undertaking to maintain high levels of
employment and utilization of productive capacity.

The figures in Table 8 reveal that production
of goods and services in the seven major industrial
countries of OECD which accounts for 90 percent of
the GDP of the entire "free world" registered an
average annual rate of growth of 4.8 percent during
the 1960's, with the GDP per capita ranging from
$1,520 for Italy to $4,660 for the United States.
Japan attained the highest growth rate of the entire group (11.3 percent) and the United Kingdom
the lowest (2.7 percent). Such a slow growth rate
has been the factor responsible for the decline of
the United Kingdom from first to fourteenth place
during the last century. The group of 11 northern
European countries, which account for only 7.3 percent of the combined OECD GDP, achieved a slightly
lower average annual rate of growth over the 1960's,
while the per capita GDP ranged from $1,040 for
Ireland to $3,230 for Sweden.

The four southern European countries, representing the developing nations in the Mediterranean
region (Spain, Portugal, Greece, and Turkey),
achieved an average annual rate of growth in GDP of
6.7 percent, or well above the average for the two
other groups of member countries. However, their
per capita GDP was well below the $1,000 level,
with Turkey in the lowest place at only $380.

Implications of the Widening Gap

Although precise comparisons are not possible
on the basis of the available statistical data, and

TABLE 8

Average Annual Rates of Growth of GDP in OECD Countries, 1960-70

	Weight	Growth Rate	Per Capita GDP (U.S. dollars at 1969 market prices)
Major Countries			
Germany	8.6	4.7	2,520
Canada	3.6	4.9	3,460
United States	53.3	4.2	4,660
France	7.3	5.6	2,770
Italy	4.1	5.7	1,520
Japan	5.4	11.3	1,630
United Kingdom	7.7	2.7	1,970
Total	90.0	4.8	
Other Northern European Countries			
Austria	0.7	4.2	1,690
Belgium	1.3	4.7	2,360
Denmark	0.7	4.7	2,860
Finland		4.5	1,940
Ireland	0.2	3.9	1,040
Iceland	0.1	4.3	1,890
Luxembourg	0.1	3.0	2,230
Norway	0.5	4.7	2,530
Netherlands	1.3	5.1	2,190
Sweden	1.4	4.5	3,230
Switzerland	1.0	4.2	3,020
Total	7.3	4.6	
Other Southern European Countries			
Spain	1.4	7.4	870
Greece	0.4	6.8	950
Portugal	0.3	5.7	600
Turkey	0.6	5.7	380
Total	2.7	6.7	
Total OECD	100.0	4.8	
Total OECD Europe	94.6	4.7	

Source: OECD, The Growth of Output 1960-1980: Retrospect, Prospect and Problems of Policy (Paris, December, 1970), Table 23. See also L'Observateur de l'OCDE, No. 50 (February, 1971).

in particular between the trends in the per capita
GDP of the developed and developing market economies, it is instructive to contrast the 1960 and
1968 figures for certain regions of the world. Table 9 shows the per capita GDP (at 1964 prices) for
five areas comprising 84 developing countries in
1960 and 1968. The corresponding figures for the
industrialized countries refer to the whole group
of advanced market economies of Western Europe.

It can be seen from the figures of Table 9
that, whereas the GDP per capita in the industrialized market economies went up by 34.1 percent from
1960 to 1968, the growth rate for the developing
countries over the same period was 22 percent. The
result of such disparate average annual growth
rates between the two groups of countries was to
widen the existing gap in GDP per capita by about
10 percent over a period of nine years.

TABLE 9

Per Capita GDP, 1960 and 1968
(U.S. dollars, in 1964 prices)

Area	Number of Countries	1960	1968
Developing countries			
Africa	30	108	122
Asia	15	90	105
Southern Europe	7	320	478
Latin America	25	324	374
Middle East	7	223	327
Total	84 (average)	148	181
Industrialized countries			
Western Europe	14	1,157	1,473
Total industrialized countries (average)		1,628	2,183

Source: For developing countries: World Bank,
Trends in Developing Countries (Washington, D.C.,
1970), Table 22; for industrialized countries, OECD
figures adjusted in U.S. dollars at 1964 prices.

Findings of the Pearson Commission

The data for the period 1950-70 indicate that, despite a significant measure of economic progress achieved by the developing nations over these years, especially in the field of infrastructure investment, the gap between rich and poor countries widened. This trend must be attributed to the fact that the average yearly growth rate attained by the developing nations did not exceed 4.8 percent. It is generally agreed that a growth rate of this order is inadequate for the achievement of faster economic progress.

In the light of this situation, one cannot but regard as surprising the assertion by the Pearson Commission that "the growth record (in the developing countries) has been good."[16] The justification given for this statement is even more surprising, namely that the 4.8 percent growth rate is "considerably faster than the growth rates estimated for the presently industrialised countries in the early stages of their development."[17]

Are we justified in feeling complacent about a present growth rate that only slightly exceeds that of a century ago when the water mill and the steam engine were the most advanced technological achievements of the day? Can we be content with the thought that growth rates today are slightly faster than they were in the nineteenth century when the factors of production were rudimentary and when it took 75 years for productivity to double whereas today it doubles within a mere 10 years?

Moreover, this statement by the Pearson Commission does not correspond to reality. It is even contradicted by the statistical data quoted in the Commission's report, since on the same page one reads that the average annual growth rate was about 4 percent in the United States between 1820 and 1850, some 4 percent in Japan between 1876 and 1900, and 2.7 percent in Germany between 1850 and 1880. If developing countries managed to achieve a 4

percent growth rate a century ago, can one seriously regard the 4.8 percent growth rate attained by
the now developing countries as "satisfactory,"
particularly when even this low rate is not reached
by all of them? How can one overlook the fact that
during the early age of industrialization population increased at only half the present rate and
hence the growth in the per capita GDP was appreciably faster than today? Of course, the Pearson
Commission does not overlook this fact. It underlines that the accelerating rate of population
growth in the developing countries kept the rate of
growth of income per capita down to an average of
2-2.5 percent per year. The Commission does not
provide statistical data as to the growth of per
capita income during the preceding century, although
it asserts that this growth (2-2.5 percent) "also
compares favorably with the early experience of the
industrialized countries," implying that they are
almost equal. However, the United States data reveal a 2.5 percent growth of income per capita per
year between 1850 and 1900. In the same report,
one reads that from 1850 to 1950 per capita income
in Europe and North America rose by an average of
2 percent per year.

     Moreover, it should be stressed that the rate
of growth of per capita income on an average of 2.4
percent from 1950 does not apply to the entire
group of developing nations. Exclusive of the
People's Republic of China, 22 percent of the total
population of the developing world lives in regions
that have a per capita income growth rate of less
than 1 percent per year, and 48 percent in countries with a 1-3 percent growth rate. Only 30 percent of the population of the developing nations
has achieved a per capita income growth rate above
2 percent per year.[18]

     Despite this situation, the Pearson Commission
regards the record of development as satisfactory
and does not appear unduly perturbed by the prospect that, at the present rate of growth, per capita income will increase only fourfold over the next

60 to 70 years. For instance, India, Pakistan, and
Indonesia, with a per capita income per year of
less than $100, will by the year 2030 have reached
the level of only $400, or appreciably less than
the $500 that is even now regarded as the dividing
line between developed and developing nations. Can
one pretend to be satisfied that such a meager improvement in these low-income countries will assure
their inhabitants a certain measure of socioeconomic betterment even at the exclusion of a "wide
range of effective choice"?

It is indeed somewhat strange that the members
of the Pearson Commission should not appear more
concerned about the crucial problem created by the
strikingly slow growth rates in the developing
countries, and that they should not feel it incum-
bent upon themselves to put forward proposals for
drastic and even revolutionary policy measures to
cope with this urgent situation. Instead, they
have contented themselves with collecting data and
formulating optimistic statements coupled with
vague policy recommendations dispersed in volumi-
nous text. However, one must admit that the analysis of the problems associated with the developing
world (such as aid, external indebtedness, foreign
trade, and raw materials) has yielded a series of
interesting proposals that, if adopted, could contribute to a more rapid growth of the developing
countries. These sometimes admirable proposals
lose some of their forcefulness for two reasons:
(1) they are not included in the section of the report dealing with the outline of a general strategy
and (2) certain of the recommendations for action,
notably those regarding the financing of economic
development, did not receive the unanimous support
of the Commission.

On the whole, even though not sharing all the
views of certain severe critics of the work of the
Pearson Commission, one cannot but feel that the
Commission did not fulfill the task set it by its
sponsors. In the opinion of an authority on the
problems of developing countries, Harry G. Johnson,

"the Pearson Report, in short, may be a tombstone
rather than a milestone in the evolution of a developing world economy."[19]

A number of international commissions dealing
with the problem of development do not seem to share
the opinions of the Pearson Commission.

In submitting his annual report in 1969, Raul
Prebish, then Secretary General of UNCTAD, stressed
the point that "Outside some remarkable exceptions,
the developing countries are drifting away" and
added: "It is proper to arrest immediately this
alarming process and reverse it."[20] The Secretary
General of the United Nations, U Thant, in his mes-
sage to the forty-third session of the Economic and
Social Council in the summer of 1967, said, inter
alia: "The anxiety I expressed mid-way of the Development Decade was unfortunately borne out by the
disappointing evolution of the first two years."[21]
Furthermore, Edwin M. Martin, President of the Development Assistance Committee (DAC), in his report
for the year 1969, explains the reasons for the
disappointment of the developing countries and emphasizes that these countries have now reached a
critical stage that is expected to be decisive.[22]
Again, the former Director General of the International Labor Organization (ILO), David Morse, re-
porting to the International Labor Conference in
1970, gave prominence to the problem of poverty and,
while recognizing the progress achieved over the
last twenty years, laid special emphasis on the
fact that the huge development effort had not, thus
far, resulted in any significant improvement in the
living standards of the greater part of the inhabitants of the world.[23]

These statements and findings, even if expressed in varying form, arrive at similar fundamental conclusions. They all serve to underline
the urgency of the problem of underdevelopment and
the need for drastic measures to cope with the
alarming situation. The problem of underdevelopment will assume an even more serious aspect if the

growth rates of the last two decades do not improve.
All the indications are that the situation may be
expected to deteriorate unless the present development policies undergo a radical change in their
strategic objectives, especially since, as will be
discussed in Chapter 2, the population explosion
will create new and acute problems in the not too
far distant future.

NOTES

1.   World Economy Survey, 1969-1970 (New York:
United Nations, 1971), p. 1.

2.   The social aspect of development was
stressed during the last few years in both the
United Nations surveys and various other reports
drafted by committees set up in preparation of an
appropriate international development strategy for
the Second United Nations Development Decade.   See
World Economic Survey, 1968 (New York: United Nations, 1969).   See also, and in particular, the report of a group of experts who convened under the
chairmanship of Gunnar Myrdal in Stockholm in September, 1969: Policy and Social Planning in National Development (New York: United Nations, 1970,
Sales No. E.CN 5.445).   The necessity for social
orientation of development is explicitly admitted
in the proposals prepared by the Committee for Development Planning at its sixth session from January 5-15, 1970, sometimes called the Tinbergen Report after the Chairman of the Committee, Jan Tinbergen.   The report concludes that the process of
development should be viewed in terms of fundamental structural changes and as much with reference
to concepts and methods appropriate to planned social transformation as those customary to economic
analysis and policy-making.   Hence, "the distinction often made between economic and social objectives is not a very meaningful one to draw."   See
Towards Accelerated Development: Proposals for the
Second United Nations Development Decade (New York:

United Nations, 1970, Sales No. E.70.II.A.2), p. 5.
The proposals of the Tinbergen Report served as the
basis for the final decisions with regard to the
Second United Nations Development Decade taken by
the General Assembly at its twenty-fifth session
(October 24, 1970).

3.   Tinbergen Report, op. cit., p. 18. Moreover, the Myrdal Report, op. cit., stresses the
significance of the concept of "planned social
transformation" and considers it an effective instrument of policies designed to influence the behavior of individuals and justify expenditures on
social services (paragraphs 17, 18, and 19).

4.   S. I. Palmar has prepared several studies
of development problems under the auspices of the
World Council of Churches. In a summary of his
findings published in the FAO Revue CERES (July/
August 1970) he stresses the fact that the peoples
of the Third World "demand above all social justice
and dignity."

5.   "Mankind faces the choice between change
by law and lawless change." Wilfred Jenks, Director General of the ILO, in his address to the
fifty-fourth International Labor Conference, Geneva,
June, 1970.

6.   In recent years, economic theory in the
development field has made considerable strides and
the flow of empirical studies of the development
process has reached "torrential proportions," to
quote Charles P. Kindleberger, a leading authority
on development economics. Here is a selection from
the most recent publications: I. Albertini, Les
mécanismes du sous-développement (Paris: Editions
Ovrieres, 1967); P. Bairoch, Diagnostic de l'évolu-
tion économique du tiers-monde, 1900-1968 (Paris:
Gauthier-Villar, 1970), A. B. Batchelder, The Economics of Poverty (New York: John Wiley, 1968);
T. Bauer and B. S. Yamey, The Economics of Under-
Developed Countries (Cambridge: Cambridge University Press, 1957); J. Bhagwati, L'économie des pays

sous-développés (Paris: Hachette, 1966); J. de
Castro, Géopolitique de la faim (Paris: Editions
Oyrieres, 1971); J. Freyssinet, Le concept du sous-
développement (Paris, 1970); C. Furtado, Developpe-
ment et sous-développement (Paris: Presses Universitaires de France, 1966); M. Guernier, La dernière
chance du tiers-monde (Paris: Laffout, 1968);
A. O. Hirschman, The Strategy of Economic Development (New Haven: Yale University Press, 1959); D.
Horowitz, Hemispheres North and South: Economic
Disparity among Nations (Baltimore: Johns Hopkins
Press, 1966); H. G. Johnson, Economic Policies Towards Less Developed Countries (Washington, D.C.:
Brookings Institution, 1967); P. Moussa, Les nations
prolétaires (Paris: Presses Universitaires de
France, 1960); H. Myint, The Economics of the Devel-
oping Countries (London, 1964); G. Myrdal, The Chal-
lenge of World Poverty (New York: Pantheon Books,
1970); G. Myrdal, Economic Theory and Under-Developed
Regions (London: Duckworth, 1957); L. Pearson, The
Crisis of Development (London: Pall Mall Press,
1970); F. Perroux, L'economie des jeunes nations
(Paris: Presses Universitaires de France, 1962);
J. Pincus, Trade, Aid and Development: The Rich
and Poor Nations (New York: McGraw-Hill, 1967);
D. Seers and L. JoyLed, Development in a Divided
World (London: Pelican, 1971); B. Ward, Rich and
Poor Nations (New York: W. W. Norton, 1962).

7.   Robert S. McNamara, elected late in 1968
President of the International Bank for Reconstruction and Development, invited Lester B. Pearson,
former Prime Minister of Canada and recipient of
the Nobel Prize for Peace, to form a Commission to
"study the consequences of twenty years of development assistance, assess the results, clarify the
errors and propose the policies which will work
better in the future."   Mr. Pearson invited seven
experts from different countries to join him on the
Commission. They are: Sir Edward Boyle (United
Kingdom), Roberto de Oliveira Campos (Brazil), C.
Douglas Dillion (United States), Wilfried Guth
(Federal Republic of Germany), W. Arthur Lewis
(Jamaica), Robert E. Marjolin (France), and Saburo

Okita (Japan). The report was published under the title <u>Partners in Development: Report of the Commission on International Development</u> (New York: Praeger Publishers, 1969).

8. In Secretariat of the Economic Commission for Europe, <u>Economic Survey of Europe in 1969</u>, an estimate is undertaken of per capita real income levels in European countries, east and west, in 1965. A new method is used to find appropriate non-monetary indicators that correlate well with per capita income levels. The criteria of selection applied were: (1) since each indicator yields its own "individual" estimate of income level, selected indicators should be available for all the countries under study, (2) that the indicators be comparable between countries, i.e., they should not differ qualitatively, and (3) that the indicators cover a wide range of social and economic aspects of development. The 21 indicators chosen finally include per capita consumption of steel, cement, sulfuric acid, electric energy, plastic materials, textile yarns (kg./head), animal proteins and cereals (grams/day), and sugar (kg./head); milk yield per cow (liters); active population in agriculture (percentages) and TV sets, telephones, and passenger cars per 1,000 inhabitants. See <u>Economic Survey of Europe in 1969</u> (Geneva: United Nations, 1970), pp. 146-47. For details about the method employed, see Chapter 4 "International Comparisons of Real Incomes, Capital Formation and Consumption (Note on a Methodological Experiment)," pp. 139-49. Although the method of calculation used by the Economic Commission for Europe is admittedly meaningful for international comparisons on a uniform basis, it is not suitable in estimating the global world income. Moreover, the attempt by the Statistical Commission of the United Nations to establish a relation between the two methods of calculating real incomes did not produce any concrete results. See <u>National Accounts and Balances</u> (New York: United Nations, 1969, Sales No. E.CN. 3.362.1.68).

9. The 1968 figures referred to in the Pearson Report differ slightly from our estimates.

Thus, in 1970 developing countries accounted for
12.5 percent of the GNP of the non-communist world,
as against 14.2 percent according to our calculations. See Partners in Development, op. cit., p.
24.

10. The problem of world poverty was the subject of the annual report of the International Labor Conference, fifty-fifth Session, Geneva, May,
1970. See International Labor Office, Poverty and
the Minimum Living Standards (Geneva, 1970). The
report contains significant facts and highly interesting findings about the magnitude and nature of
world poverty. Furthermore, the same subject was
considered by the United Nations with special emphasis on the distribution of national income. The
Commission for Social Development undertook a series of studies on the different aspects of the
problem of poverty. See Social Policy and the Distribution of Income in the Nation (New York: United
Nations, 1969, Sales No. 69.IV.7).

11. See de Castro, op. cit., p. 57. The
first edition of this work, already a classic, is
still topical and has been translated into 27 languages. The French text has reached the tenth edition (1971) and has been most instrumental in mobilizing public opinion and the international institutions in the struggle against world hunger.

12. All those interested in a study in depth
of the problems of poverty and economic backwardness
in Asia are advised to read the monumental work of
Gunnar Myrdal, Asian Drama: An Inquiry into the
Poverty of Nations, Twentieth Century Fund (New
York: Pantheon, 1968), Volumes I-III. In his
latest work, World Poverty, op. cit., Gunnar Myrdal
refers to the main conclusions of his study on
Asian poverty and formulates concrete proposals for
action. In the particular case of poverty in India,
the work by Tarlok Singh, Poverty and Social Change,
2nd ed. (Bombay: Orient Longmans, 1969), contains
valuable statistics and background information.
Moreover, it makes a number of significant proposals
designed to achieve a transformation of the socioeconomic structure of India.

13. See "Poverty in India," prepared by the Indian School of Political Economy, Poona, and published in Economic and Political Weekly (Bombay), January 2 and 9, 1971. For a summary and evaluation of this study, see The Economist, March 27, 1971, pp. 41-42.

14. These estimates have been prepared by the Statistical Commission of the United Nations and were quoted by the Secretary General U Thant, Portfolio for Peace (New York, 1970).

15. Partners in Development, op. cit., p. 55.

16. Ibid., p. 28.

17. Ibid., p. 27.

18. Ibid., p. 29.

19. See H. G. Johnson, The "Crisis of Aid" and the Pearson Report (Edinburgh: Edinburgh University Press, 1970).

20. See International Development Strategy for 1970 (New York: United Nations, 1969, Sales No. F.68.II.D.6), p. 1.

21. See Official Records of the Economic and Social Council, Forty-third Session, 1480th meeting.

22. See OECD, Development Assistance: Efforts and Policies of the Members of the Development Assistance Committee, 1969 Review (Paris: OECD Secretariat, 1970), p. 13.

23. International Labor Office, op. cit.

2

**POPULATION
EXPLOSION
IN THE
THIRD WORLD**

ACCELERATION OF POPULATION GROWTH

One of the salient characteristics of the developing nations is the significantly faster growth rate of their population as compared with that of the industrially advanced countries. Whereas the average yearly growth rate of world population is about 2 percent, the developed countries have shown a 1 percent rise in population as against 3 percent for the developing countries. In some of the poorer regions of the Third World, the population has been growing at an average annual rate of even more than 3 percent.

The full significance of these growth rates becomes apparent when it is realized that with a 1 percent average annual increase a country's population will double within 70 years, at 2 percent within 35 years, and at 3.5 percent within only 20 years. Assuming an average annual rate of increase of 2 percent, the population of the world must have reached about 3,584 million by 1970 and will be about 7,000 million (or twice its present size) in the year 2005. By the year 2040, always assuming a continuing growth rate of 2 percent per year, world population will have risen to about 14,000 million.

In other words, a child born today will, if he
lives to the age of 70, then find himself a unit in
a world population of 14 billion, while his grand-
children will share life on this planet with some
60 billion human beings.

The human race has indeed achieved a spectacular reproduction rate. While it took as much as
1,600 years for the world's population to double between the end of the first century and the end of
the seventeenth century, and a further 150 years
from 1750 to 1900 to double once more, today the
process of doubling takes only 35 years.[1] The mortality rate has been reduced drastically in the developed regions. However, since 1950 the reduction
trend has spread to the developing nations where
the previous high mortality rates have dropped significantly. Up to as late as the nineteenth century, the mortality rate in all parts of the world
was very high and life expectancy very short.* However, during the last 150 years average life expectancy has risen from 30 to 70 years, and in the developing countries now stands at about 50 years.

The most disturbing aspect of the population
explosion is the fact that, while the fertility
rate in the developed countries steadily declined
from 3.8 percent during the period 1850-1900 to
about 1.8 percent in the 1960's, the fertility rate
in the developing countries remains as high as 4-
4.5 percent, more than twice as high as in the developed countries. The fertility rate is thus a
significant factor in any comparison between developed and developing countries.

----

*It is estimated that almost up to 1850, death
and birth rates were 3.5 percent and 4 percent respectively. After 1850, in today's developed regions of the world average mortality rates declined
to 2.8 percent and by the end of the nineteenth century stood at 1.8 percent. The mortality rate
dropped further to below 1 percent after 1950. In
the developing regions, mortality rates were reduced
from 2.2 percent during the 1950-60 period to 1.7
percent in the 1960's.

Furthermore, these largely divergent fertility rates signify that in the developed countries the process of population dynamics is less powerful since, because of the higher share and faster growth in the number of old people, the mortality rates have ceased to decline and have even gone up slightly. This situation contrasts sharply with that of the developing nations where the proportion of young persons is very high and where the mortality rates are fast declining and will fall even lower than the present level in the developed countries. As a result, the population in the developing regions as a whole is expanding at an average annual rate of 2.5 percent, and in the poorer nations by as much as 3-3.5 percent,* as against a 1 percent increase in the rich countries. It may therefore be expected, according to the forecasts of the United Nations Commission on Population, that there will be a tremendous rise in world population over several decades.

Table 10 contains data on the distribution of world population in 1970 by main groups of countries, the respective growth rates, and the number of years required for the doubling of the population. The figures in Table 10 indicate that the population of the developed market economies will double within a period ranging from 70 to 140 years, whereas in the developing regions the number of years required for a twofold increase varies from only 24 to 39 years. The two extreme cases in Table 10 are Indonesia and the United Kingdom. In the first case, the population will double within 24 years and in the second within 140 years. However, Latin America is the region with the fastest growth of population. From 63 million in 1900 it took 50 years for the population to increase by a further 100 million, while at the present rate it is expected to double within 24 years, or increase by 100 million persons every 5 years.

---

*In order to appraise the repercussions of these trends, one should take into account that in the developing regions the average annual rate of population growth was 0.3 percent from 1850 to 1000 and 0.9 percent over the 1900-50 period.

TABLE 10

Number of Years Required for Doubling of Population, by Group and Country, 1970

	Population (millions)	Births (per thousand)	Deaths (per thousand)	Annual Rate of Natural Increase	Number of Years Required for Doubling
Developing countries					
Africa	344	47	20	2.7	27
Asia	2,056	38	15	2.3	31
China	760	34	15	1.8	39
India	555	42	17	2.6	27
Indonesia	121	49	21	2.9	24
Latin America	283	38	9	2.9	24
Industrialized countries					
United States	205	18	9	1.0	70
U.S.S.R.	242	18	8	1.0	70
Western Europe	462	18	10	0.8	88
United Kingdom	56	17	12	0.5	140
France	51	17	11	0.8	88
West Germany	58	20	12	0.6	117
Switzerland	6	17	9	1.1	63
Italy	54	18	10	0.8	88
Greece	9	18	8	0.8	88
Turkey	36	43	16	2.7	26
World	3,684	34	14	2.0	35

Source: Various U.N. publications.

52

PROJECTIONS FOR THE YEAR 2000

According to the most recent projections prepared by the United Nations Office for Population, world population as a whole, and that of the developed and developing regions, is expected to grow as shown in Table 11.

TABLE 11

Population Projections for Selected Years
(in millions)

	1970	1980	1990	2000
Developed	1,115	1,210	1,336	1,454
Developing	2,469	3,247	4,102	5,040
World	3,584	4,457	5,438	6,494

Source: Statistical Office of the United Nations, Monthly Bulletin of Statistics, April, 1971. According to an earlier study, prepared by the Department of Economic and Social Affairs of the United Nations entitled World Population Prospects as Assessed in 1963 (New York: United Nations, 1966), three sets of future estimates were presented for the evolution of the world's population, namely, the "medium," "high," and "low" variants. In general, only one set of estimates corresponding to the "medium" variant was presented for countries. However, it must be emphasized that future trends outside the limits of the "high" and "low" variants are by no means impossible (p. 6). For the year 2000, total world population was estimated at 6,994 million, 6,130 million and 5,449 million according to the "high," "medium," and "low" variants, respectively (p. 15, Table 4.3). The 1971 revision of population estimates shows an excess of 364 million over the medium variant used in the 1963 world population projections.

According to these projections, based on a
medium growth variant, by the end of the present
century more than two-thirds of the world's population, or more exactly 77.5 percent, will be concentrated in the developing regions, as against 69.9
percent in 1970. These trends appear quite realistic since, of the 66 million increase in world population in 1970, only 9.5 million was added to the
population of the developed countries, as against
an increase of 56.5 million in the developing countries. By the year 2000, Asia alone, exclusive of
Japan, will have a population totaling 3,645 million,
or 60 million more than the present population of
the entire world. Thus, 56.5 percent of the world's
population will be living in regions that are considered to be extremely poor. By contrast, the developed regions will account in the year 2000 for
22.5 percent of the world's population as compared
with 36.2 percent in 1920. As a result of these
projected far-reaching shifts in the population
structure by the year 2000, more than three persons
out of four will then be living in today's developing regions. Figure 3 shows clearly the distribution of world population according to a threefold
classification of its regions. Figure 4 shows the
future evolution of population.

In the light of the foregoing statistics and
projections, the population explosion must be seen
as constituting the most serious challenge of our
times and as threatening to upset the world balance.
The present situation is bound to assume more alarming proportions since these immense additions to
the human race will be concentrated in regions
where two-thirds of mankind already live in conditions of abject poverty, with insufficient food,
primitive housing, and inadequate medical care.

THE OUTLOOK FOR CONTROLLING POPULATION
GROWTH IN THE THIRD WORLD

One of the dominant issues today is whether and
how far the world's resources will prove adequate to

FIGURE 3

Distribution of World Population, 1970

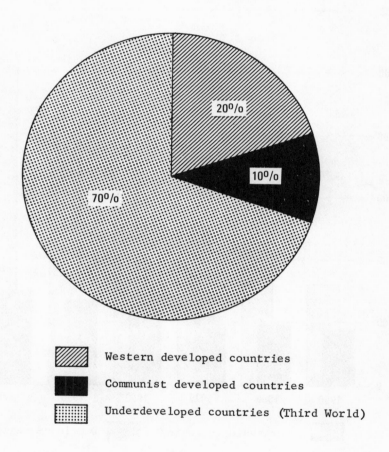

FIGURE 4

Future Evolution of World Population
(in millions)

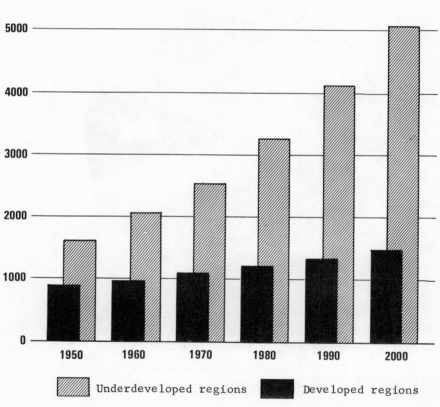

feed the entire human race in the near future, given
the present rates of growth in world population and
production.

The FAO, together with several other international agencies, has been studying this crucial
question. In addition to producing a series of
studies on the problem of world food supplies, FAO
in 1960 launched a campaign against hunger designed
to induce governments, various agencies, industrial-
ists, schools and universities, youth organizations,
and, in general, all sections of society in all
countries to unite their efforts in a concerted
struggle to eradicate hunger and misery.[2] Moreover,
various personalities of world repute have spared
no effort to warn the governments of all countries
of the peril that is fast approaching should present
growth rates in production and population persist
indefinitely. Among the leading authorities on the
subject, mention should be made in particular of
Josué de Castro, former president of FAO. His name
is closely associated with the campaign against hunger. Mr. de Castro has repeatedly stressed in his
writings and lectures how desperately urgent the
problem of hunger is, and how most people who do
not suffer from hunger avoid mentioning this un-
pleasant subject. In numerous works, Alfred Sauvy,
the distinguished sociologist, has dealt constructively with the world's demographic problem and has
strongly condemned the callous indifference of the
rich countries in squandering precious resources on
nonproductive and useless projects.

In addition, two international conferences organized by the United Nations, the first in Rome in
1954 and the second in Belgrade in 1965, discussed
all aspects of the world population problem.

Despite a certain amount of progress achieved
during the last few years in the production of food
and a wider public awareness of the issues at stake,
the demographic problem has lost none of its acute-
ness.

While it is true that, in the strict sense of
the word, there are no cases of actual famine, nevertheless 10-15 percent of the world's population
still goes hungry. Moreover, almost half the inhabitants of the developing countries suffer from
malnutrition or chronic undernourishment. The danger gap is expected to widen in the near future as
a result of the increase in population. Hence,
there is widespread pessimism about the future of
mankind. At the present rate of growth, some 70 to
80 million persons annually will swell the number
of people to be fed while the world will have
reached the limits of resource capacity. Then famine and misery will definitely check the present
population explosion. Some demographers even went
so far as to assert, during the 1965 Belgrade Congress on Population, that population growth creates
the danger of an immediate social disaster if the
production and distribution of farm products should
fail to keep up with the world's minimum food requirements.[3] According to FAO estimates, the abolition of hunger and a slight improvement in dietary
levels requires a twofold increase in food output
by 1980 and a more than threefold increase by the
end of the century.

Unfortunately, experience of the working of
food production policies during the first Development Decade cannot be regarded as encouraging. In
his report for 1970, A. A. H. Boerma, Director General of FAO, makes the point that, although the
present situation is not as alarming as that in
1965 and 1966, the danger has far from disappeared.
Demand for food by the developing nations may reasonably be expected to increase at an average annual
rate of 4 percent up to 1985. The world must therefore be prepared, warns Mr. Boerma, to undertake a
long, arduous, and extremely costly struggle if hunger and malnutrition are to be defeated.

However, according to the 1970 figures world
production of foodstuffs went up by only 2 percent,
that is, at a rate equivalent to the growth of population. Therefore, it is clear that the quantity of

available food per capita has remained unchanged.
If the present situation persists, the threat of
undernourishment will be increased and the danger
of social conflict accentuated.

Whereas FAO looks for a solution of the problem of world hunger primarily in a more rapid increase of world production of goods and services,
other international agencies are inclined to give
priority to birth control as a means of dealing
with the demographic problem. As early as 1949 the
Royal Commission on Population in the United Kingdom expressed the opinion that the problem was es-
sentially one of ways and means of controlling population growth rates that were considered unaccept-
able. The Commission proposed birth control as a
solution to the problem.

Although this approach to the population problem has been endorsed by other international agencies, the results have been disappointing. In fact,
the average annual population growth rate, far from
declining, now stands at 2 percent for the world as
a whole and 2.5 percent for the developing nations,
whereas during 1945-50 the corresponding rates were
1.5 and 1.8 percent respectively.

Today, twenty years later, numerous experts
urge family planning and assign top priority to the
policies designed to check the growth of population.
Speaking at a conference of the Inter-American Press
Association in Buenos Aires in October, 1968, Robert
S. McNamara, President of IBRD, stressed the fact
that "the rapid population growth is the most serious obstacle to economic progress and social welfare
of the inhabitants." He added that the World Bank,
as a world agency, must "assign priority" to the
population problem and to the research programs designed to determine the most effective methods of
family planning and demographic control. Mr.
McNamara has elaborated the same thesis on various
subsequent occasions, and particularly in his address to the Council of Governors of the International Monetary Fund (IMF) in Copenhagen in 1971.

Furthermore, the Pearson Commission Report stresses the urgent necessity of adopting measures to mitigate the ominous implications of uncontrolled population growth.

The question now arises as to whether and how far the various administrative measures to "regulate population growth" can provide an effective solution of this crucial "population dilemma."

THE DEMOGRAPHIC PROBLEM AS A FUNCTION OF THE ECONOMIC PROBLEM

It can no longer be disputed that the present population growth rate of the Third World is far too high and must gradually be brought to a more reasonable level. Nevertheless, while priority should be given to measures designed to cope with the population explosion through family planning, there is the danger of overlooking the paramount priority that must be assigned to the task of accelerating economic development since this alone will provide a long-term solution of the demographic problem.

The assertion that the rapid population growth constitutes "the greatest obstacle to economic and social progress" is reminiscent of the famous doctrine of Thomas Robert Malthus, which was not only subsequently contradicted but totally refuted by developments in the industrialized countries. As early as 1798, Malthus had propounded the doctrine that poverty was the consequence of unchecked population growth. He drew a gloomy picture of man being born into an already overpopulated world with "no claim of right to the smallest portion of food" and warned that nature would soon restore balance through the misery of poverty.

Since the days of Malthus, events have shown that within the developed countries production of goods and services has exceeded the rate of population growth, a fact that has totally refuted his doctrine. In fact, it has been found that wealth, and not poverty, acts as a restraint on the birth rate.

Recent studies of demographic developments during the nineteenth and twentieth centuries have shown that improved living standards were associated with a simultaneous decline in both mortality and birth rates, and that a rise in per capita income had not encouraged growth in population.[4] The interdependence of social, economic, and demographic factors tends to bring about a balance between births and deaths in modern societies.

The Decline in Fertility

This problem was extensively discussed at the International Congress on Population in Belgrade in 1965. It was there agreed that a certain measure of socioeconomic progress is an essential condition for the permanent reduction of birth rates. Moreover, a number of population experts asserted that the employment of women in economic activity, together with the progress in urbanization involving the transfer of population to the modern industrial sector of the economy, results in a decline in fertility rates. It was furthermore asserted that reduction in the mortality rate leads to a voluntary reduction in the birth rate since parents are concerned with assuring their children better opportunities for advancement and a satisfactory standard of living.

Moreover, it should be emphasized that the decline in the birth rate in the developed countries took place in the absence of any government-sponsored policy of birth control and that one can therefore assume that social and economic progress operated as some sort of automatic brake gradually establishing a sound population equilibrium. These highly significant findings support the view that the socioeconomic progress of the developing countries will lead to a more rapid decline in fertility rates there than in the rich countries. The growing

awareness of parents of their responsibilities toward their children is expected to reinforce this
trend. Moreover, the extension of family planning
to larger sections of the population will have similar overall effects.

Therefore, it should be obvious that the accelerated development of the developing regions of the
world is the precondition for a reduction in birth
rates. This trend is bound to render more effective the long-term policy of controlling the population explosion and thereby minimizing the dangers
from widespread and abject poverty that otherwise
would inevitably afflict mankind. Therefore, we
may assert, in unison with several experts on economic development that, without underestimating the
importance of family planning, the overriding priority should be assigned to socioeconomic progress as
the real answer to the present challenge of population explosion.[5]

It is possible that the family planning programs may cause a certain decline in fertility
rates. However, according to a study by the Population Council of Washington, it is doubtful whether
these programs tend to accelerate the fall in fertility without concomitant changes in other areas,
such as massive improvements in education facilities, growth in employment opportunities, and,
above all, a rise in the living levels of the population. Hence, a family planning program should be
considered as one of the policy measures within the
context of an overall development strategy.[6]

The Case of The People's
Republic of China

Thanks to an imaginative policy, the People's
Republic of China succeeded in reducing the growth
rate of its population by almost one-half within a
period of fifteen years. Whereas during the last
fifty years China's population increased at an
average annual rate of about 2.5 percent, its present growth rate is less than 1.7 percent annually.

Moreover, according to the United Nations estimates, China's population is expected to increase by about 1.5 percent per annum over the period 1980-2000. The program of birth control in the People's Republic of China is a combination of various contraceptive devices, inducements to avoid early marriages, and a policy designed to assure to the population a steady improvement in its material and cultural standard of life. The experience of China appears to justify a more optimistic view of the world population problem, provided the poorer regions of the globe achieve faster socioeconomic progress for their inhabitants.

By contrast, there is a favorable response to the propaganda for birth control in the industrially advanced countries of the West, where population already grows at a very slow rate. The experts at the Strasbourg Conference on Population (September, 1971) stressed the steady aging of Europe's population and the progressive decline in its fertility rates.

On the other hand, we are constantly assured by experts that the world has at its disposal potentially inexhaustible material resources adequate to meet, after the end of the century, the needs of the world population even if it continues to grow at the present rate.[7]

THE SQUANDERING OF WEALTH

Are the rich nations willing to embark upon a policy of international cooperation or do they propose to go on squandering the world's resources as they are doing at present? Is not all this wastefulness a crime against humanity? In this context, one must subscribe to the views of Alfred Sauvy:

> If a man could stand up and speak
> aloud on behalf of a billion human
> beings, he would, without regard to
> either Marx or Malthus, address the

developed countries as follows: "You,
the rich, who possess three-quarters
of the wealth of the globe, are crim-
inally wasting that wealth. Whatever
your internal differences, they are
insignificant compared with the lives
of over a billion human beings. A generation ago guns were given priority
over butter. The choice today lies
between your guns and our butter, or
more precisely, between your rockets
and our daily bread. For it is our
bread you are squandering, leaving us
with the prospect of possibly no
bread at all tomorrow. If one day
catastrophe befalls our planet, and
if any historian survives to record
it, he will hold you accountable for
the most serious mistake any human
being has committed on this earth.
The crimes of a Caligula, an Attila,
or a Hitler, are insignificant in comparison with that which you are now
preparing to perpetrate."[8]

Since 1963 when Alfred Sauvy gave that dramat-
ic warning, the situation has further deteriorated.
The number of poor people has exceeded one billion
while the wasteful use of resources by the rich nations in unproductive expenditure has reached fan-
tastic proportions. Between 1960 and 1970, the
gross national income of the rich countries, exclusive of the communist world, rose by $918 billion.*
Over the same period, so-called development assistance went up by no more than $22 billion, of which
only $7 billion represented "grants." To a large
extent, the increase in GNP was absorbed by military and space travel expenditure that, within

----

*In 1970, the combined GNP of the industrial-
ized DAC member countries totaled $1,830 billion
as against $910 billion in 1960.

the 1960's, reached the staggering amount of $275 billion.*

According to these figures, about $30 out of every $100 of the annual growth of GNP in the rich countries between 1960 and 1970 was absorbed by an increase in the already vast military expenditure, whereas a meager $0.80 was devoted to providing real aid to the developing nations.

The outlook becomes even more ominous when the developed communist countries are included since their development assistance is much inferior to that of the market economies while the level of their military expenditure during the 1960's was not less than $150 billion.

During the 1960's, the developed countries as a whole--that is, both the market economy and the centrally planned developed countries--spent the vast sum of $425 billion on armaments. Moreover, for the year 1970 alone the combined military expenditure of all countries of the world was on the order of $207 billion, according to United Nations estimates.[9]

This sum corresponds to about 62 percent of the GNP of all developing nations or one-third of the total investment expenditure of the world as a whole.

Do we realize how vast would be the beneficial effects on the prospects of mankind if these enormous human and material resources could be devoted

---

*Military expenditure by the OECD member countries, inclusive of the United States and Canada, rose from $61.5 billion in 1960 to $110 billion in 1969. According to our estimates, military expenditure in 1970 should be on the order of $118 billion approximately, while the annual increase over the decade totals $275 billion.

to promoting more rapid socioeconomic progress
among the world's peoples?

Apart from the general issue of disarmament,
which constitutes a highly desirable long-term objective, if only two-thirds of the increase of
about $300 billion in defense expenditure during
the 1960's had been devoted to fairly distributed
and effectively utilized productive investment, a
minimum additional income of $90 billion would have
been generated.[10] The impact on world social and
economic progress would have been considerable.
Moreover, this additional wealth, if used to stimulate production and improve living standards, would
have served as an effective factor in the fight
against inflation. It must not be overlooked that
the underlying cause of today's inflation, which is
turning into a chronic disease, is the inadequacy
of productive investment. As long as enormous
amounts of resources are consumed in unproductive
expenditure on armaments and space travel, inflationary pressures will increase while social peace
will be permanently imperilled. Whatever the "economic ramifications" of military and space research
expenditure, it is a fallacy to assert that such
expenditure constitutes a significant factor in the
acceleration of economic growth. Japan serves as a
typical illustration. With military expenditure,
as a percentage of GNP, kept at a very low level
during the 1960's, that country's economy achieved
a record growth rate whereas the United States,
with a much greater share of resources devoted to
military expenditure, registered only a modest rate
of growth during the same period. Furthermore, the
dominant role that research is made to play in military and space projects leads to imbalance in the
overall research and development effort and to an
uneconomical utilization of research achievements.[11]
The U.S.S.R. faces a similar problem since it de-
votes a large part of its GNP to military expenditure and space exploration.

What appreciable signs are there of the realization of that international cooperation of which

there has been so much talk in recent years? Can
the rich nations long remain secluded in their
luxurious "club," indifferent to the problem created
by a rapidly growing world population, a great majority of whom live in abject poverty and are de-
manding elementary justice for all peoples in the
distribution of material well-being?

Can such an alarming and contradictory situation as exists today be allowed to continue without
provoking violent reactions and even bloody conflicts?

NOTES

1. World population has registered the following growth since the seventeenth century (in millions):   1650, 508; 1750, 711; 1850, 1,131; 1900,
1,590; 1950, 2,516; 1970, 3,592. World Bank,
Trends in Developing Countries (Washington, D.C.,
1970).

2. See The State of Food and Agriculture 1970
(Rome: FAO, 1970).

3. See World Population: Challenge to Development (New York: United Nations, 1966, Sales No.
E.66.XIII.4).

4. The American economist Simon Kuznets, a
leading authority in the field of quantitative
studies of the complex growth process and winner
of the 1971 Nobel prize for economics, has estimated population changes in seventeen countries
during the nineteenth century. He has proved that
improved nutritional and public health levels resulted in a decline in mortality rates with a simultaneous fall in birth rates. Mr. Kuznets computed rates of growth in population and per capita
incomes in Economic Growth of Nations (Cambridge,
Mass.:   Harvard University Press, 1971).

5. In his address on the occasion of the
twenty-fifth anniversary of the FAO on November 25,
1970, Pope Paul VI reiterated the opposition of the
Church to family planning and emphasized that
"birth control cannot be the solution of underdevelopment."

6. See Gavin W. Jones, "The Economic Effect
of Declining Fertility in Less Developed Countries"
(New York: Population Council, February, 1969).

7. See Papers presented to the Belgrade Congress, a summary of which is contained in United
Nations, World Population: Challenge to Development (New York, 1966). Moreover, Colin Clark in
his work Plenty or Famine (French translation
Abondance ou famine [Paris: Stock, 1971]) main-
tains that the world's arable land could feed 33
billion people, that is, ten times the present
world population.

8. Alfred Sauvy, Malthus et les deux Marx
(Paris: Denoël, 1963), p. 231.

9. The most recent figures are given in a
United Nations press release (No. 1971/282, November 9, 1971) on a report on the "Economic and Social Consequences of Arms Race and Military Expenditures." The report, prepared for the Secretary-
General by 14 consultant experts and placed before
the General Assembly at its 1972 session, discusses
the opportunities lost by nations, as a result of
the arms race, in public services, health, education, housing, and now the protection of the human
environment. At the international level, the arms
race "inhibits co-operation and prevents countries
from combining their forces in a united effort to
deal effectively with the development problem on
the scale required." As to the costs involved,
the report says that the arms race consumed nearly
$1.9 billion during the 1960's. If annual ex-
penditures continue at their present rate, a level
of $300-350 billion (at 1970 prices) might well be
reached by the end of the 1970's. Total outlay

for the decade would then be $750 billion more than
was spent in the 1960's.

The body of the report consists of five
closely related sections dealing with (1) "The Qual-
itative Aspects of the Arms Race," (2) "The Arms
Race in Terms of Resources," (3) "The Dynamics of
Military Research and Development," (4) "The National Consequences of the Arms Race and Military
Expenditures," and (5) "The International Consequences of the Arms Race and Military Expenditures."
The unanimous conclusions of the experts were summed
up in the report as follows:

1. A substantial reduction in the military
expenditures of all countries, particularly those
whose military expenditures are highest, should be
brought about as soon as possible. The sooner concrete measures of disarmament, particularly of nuclear disarmament, are achieved and the arms race
is thereby halted and reversed, the faster will be
the progress toward the goal of general and complete disarmament.

2. Regardless of their size or their
stage of development, all countries share the responsibility of taking steps that will help achieve
this goal.

3. A halt in the arms race and a significant reduction in military expenditures would help
the social and economic development of all countries
and would increase the possibilities for providing
additional aid to developing countries.

4. In order to draw the attention of the
governments and peoples of the world to the direction the arms race is taking, the Secretary-General
should keep the facts under periodic review.

10. According to OECD, the different estimates
on apparent productivity of a $1 investment in the
five largest countries (France, Germany, Italy,
United Kingdom, United States), although not always
significant at the usual 5 percent confidence level,
are all grouped fairly closely around the value of
$.30. In Japan, however, investment is much more
productive. See OECD, The Growth of Output 1960-
1980: Retrospect, Prospect and Problems of Policy
(Paris, December, 1970), p. 256.

11. The Brooks Report of OECD, <u>Science, Growth
and Society: A New Perspective</u> (Paris, August, 1971),
underlines the negative correlation between military
expenditures and economic growth and concludes that
the predominance of military research leads to an
imbalanced utilization of the results of research
by creating serious bottlenecks.

3

THE MAIN CAUSES
OF ECONOMIC
BACKWARDNESS
IN THE THIRD WORLD

GAPS IN THE DEVELOPMENT OF
THE THIRD WORLD

Although the growth rates achieved by the developing countries during the two decades 1950-70
cannot be regarded as satisfactory, the substantial
measure of progress made by these countries in some
important sectors of socioeconomic activity should
not be underestimated.

In the first place, most of the developing nations have engaged in an extensive program of infrastructure projects (energy, transport, communications, and so forth) designed to have a long-term
accelerating effect on the overall rate of economic
development. Substantial progress also has been
made in the sector of industry. The establishment
of domestic industries has increased the supply of
home-produced manufactures of products that previously had to be imported. Moreover, certain export-
oriented industries have contributed toward the
fuller utilization of domestic raw materials, hitherto exported unprocessed. According to recent estimates, developing countries themselves produce
about 60 per cent of the consumer goods they require,

40 to 50 percent of the semifinished products, and 20 to 30 percent of the capital goods. A major effort is being made in the field of development financing, and 85 percent of investment expenditure is now being met out of domestic saving.

Agriculture, still the major sector of economic activity in the developing countries, is making progress with the introduction of modern techniques but, although this is resulting in an improvement in crop yields, food production is still increasing at a rate slower than the rate of population growth. The progress achieved during the last few years supports the optimistic forecasts by experts, provided the so-called "green revolution" can accelerate the realization of its wider objectives. A further encouraging development is the striking increase in the number of children now receiving school education. The number of pupils enrolled has doubled, or in many cases even tripled, since 1950. However, the rapid increase in the school-age population has created new and formidable difficulties.

However, the vital precondition for progress is the increasing comprehension by the developing countries of the nature and magnitude of the problems of development, and a more resolute determination to seek their solution by the pursuit of a drastic socioeconomic policy during the next decades.

The developing nations are fully conscious of the urgent necessity to take more effective steps to mobilize domestic material and financial resources, to contain inflationary pressures, and to effect a more equitable distribution of incomes. Action along these lines is expected to accelerate development within the framework of social and economic stability.

The Lack of Rigorous Plan Implementation

Despite the appreciable progress achieved, growth rates could have been faster if developing

countries had been capable of applying a more
rigorous development policy and if their plans had
been better prepared and implemented. Again, a
more socially orientated policy, more efficient administration, greater utilization of modern techniques, and better trained manpower would have contributed significantly to the acceleration of socioeconomic development.

In some cases domestic resources have been in-
efficiently used, while foreign aid frequently has
been squandered on projects utterly unrelated to
economic development. The growing skepticism in
certain industrially advanced countries, and notably
in the United States, about the effectiveness of
foreign aid is the direct result of the misuse of
both external and domestic resources by a number of
developing nations.[1]

Again, certain developing countries seemed to
assume that the abolition of foreign domination
would automatically open the way to prosperity.
These countries were not always aware of the causes
of their actual state of economic stagnation nor of
the nature and magnitude of the obstacles to development. Consequently, they failed to adopt the required radical policy measures or to induce the
broad masses of the population to participate actively in the national development effort. Hence
the ensuing climate of popular discontent and im-
patience at the slow progress.

Social unrest and strife are inevitable if the
authorities of the developing countries fail to
make use of the available domestic resources and
thereby prove incapable of satisfying the legitimate aspirations of their people. It should never
be forgotten that the process of development involves far-reaching changes in the socioeconomic,
institutional, and cultural structure of a country,
and thereby affects the pattern of national behavior and may cause a series of troubles that can
endanger the unity of a people.

The Lack of Social Orientation

Therefore, the objectives of a development
policy cannot be attained within the context of a
static sociopolitical structure. Emergence from
the state of underdevelopment must be viewed as a
comprehensive long-term social process. As stated
earlier, it is increasingly realized that, to
achieve a rapid rate of growth in a manner acceptable to all sections of the population, there must
be adoption of policy measures that are explicitly
designed to transform and improve existing social
conditions.

It would be folly for today's low-income countries to base their development policy on the classical economic precepts of the nineteenth century.
The entire development effort must be designed and
implemented in the light of the concepts and experience of the second half of the twentieth century.

Developing countries are inclined to put part
of the blame for their backwardness on the policies
of the rich industrialized countries, particularly
their policies concerning imports and development
aid. These two major areas of policy are considered below.

COMMERCIAL POLICIES INHIBITING THE
DEVELOPMENT OF THE THIRD WORLD

The assertion that foreign trade policy is a
major instrument in national development applies
particularly in the case of the developing countries. For these countries, exports constitute almost the only source of foreign exchange earnings
with which to finance a steady growth in imports
of the goods and services that are indispensable to
the process of economic development. However, the
export sector of developing countries shows a high
degree of instability since the exports consist
mainly of primary products, sometimes to the extent

of 90 percent. On the average, developing countries
rely for one-half of their export earnings on a
single commodity. Moreover, given price instability
and the lack of export diversification, it is not
surprising that developing countries have benefited
only to a limited extent from the postwar expansion
in world trade. Therefore, it was natural that at
various international conferences, and above all
that of UNCTAD, the export problem of these countries should be the major subject under consideration.

Decline in the Developing Countries' Share in World Trade

Since 1950, world trade has shown a spectacular expansion. Between 1960 and 1969, world exports
rose from $128 billion to $272 billion, or at an
average annual rate of 9 percent as against 6.4 percent for the priod 1955-59. For the years 1968 and
1969, the average annual rate of growth jumped to
13.6 percent.[2] The developing nations of course
participated in this expansion of world trade, although to a lesser extent than the developed countries. Thus, for the period 1950-69 the average
annual rate of increase in the value of exports of
developing countries was only 4.7 percent, compared
to 8.7 percent for the developed countries. The
distribution of world exports by major economic
areas in the years 1950, 1960, and 1969, at 1969
prices, is shown in Table 12.

From the data in Table 12 it can be seen that
the share of the advanced market economies in world
export rose from 60.8 percent in 1950 to 71.2 percent in 1969, whereas the share of the developing
countries during the same period declined from
31.2 percent to 17.9 percent. The centrally planned
economies increased their share from 8 percent to
10.9 percent.

This spectacular fall in the developing nations' percentage share of world export trade--a
fall that was accentuated in the course of 1970--

can be ascribed, to a large extent, to the dominant
role of the developed countries in determining the
evolution and pattern of the international flow of
goods and services (see Figure 5). These countries
account for as much as 80 percent of world GNP.
The resumption of vigorous economic activity, in
the United States and West Germany, for example,
during 1968 led to a rise in imports of 23.4 percent and 16.1 percent, respectively, above the 1967
level. In absolute figures, the value of imports
by these two major industrial countries rose by
$9.1 billion, a figure that represents 46 percent
of the aggregate expansion of imports by all advanced market economies. The unfavorable trends of
the last two decades may be expected to persist as
long as the developing nations remain in their
present state of economic backwardness.

TABLE 12

Distribution of World Exports for
Selected Years, 1950-69

	1950	1960	1969	Value (millions of U.S. dollars at 1969 prices)
	(percentage)			
Market economies				
Developed	60.8	66.8	71.2	193.4
Developing	31.2	21.3	17.9	38.7
Centrally planned	8.0	11.9	10.9	29.5
Total	100.0	100.0	100.0	261.6

Source: General Agreement on Tariffs and
Trade (GATT), International Trade in 1969 (Geneva,
1970); Olivier Long (Director General of GATT),
Réflections sur les mutations du commerce international (Geneva, 1970).

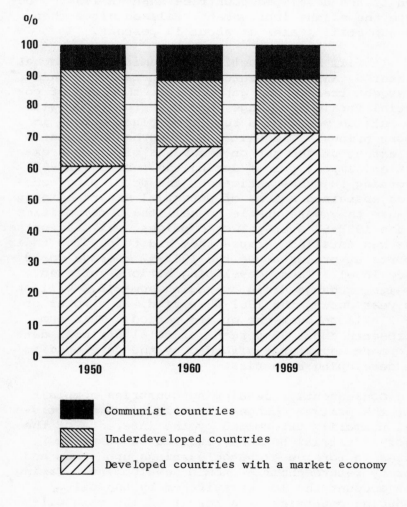

FIGURE 5

Evolution of World Trade, 1950, 1960, and 1969

Communist countries

Underdeveloped countries

Developed countries with a market economy

The dominant position of the developed countries within the world economy has caused a deterioration in the terms of trade of the developing nations. Price fluctuations have resulted in a significant loss of foreign exchange earnings for this latter group of countries. At the first development conference in Geneva in 1964, it was estimated that in 1962 the terms of trade of the developing countries were 15 percent less favorable in relation to the developed countries than in 1954.[3] Despite the slight improvement realized since then, the gap still stands at about 13 percent.

It will be instructive to examine in somewhat greater detail the nature and importance of this divergent trend. The gap reflects the loss of potential foreign exchange earnings from trade with the outside world as a result of fluctuations in export prices. The United Nations has calculated the extent of the gap on the basis of average export and import prices during the period 1953-57. According to these estimates, the developing countries sustained a loss of potential export earnings because they were unable to sell their commodities at the 1953-57 average world prices, while a further loss was entailed because they had to pay for their imports at prices above the 1953-57 average world price level. Thus, developing nations suffered a foreign exchange drain averaging some $2.2 billion per year during the 1961-66 period, or a total of $13.3 billion over the entire period. This sum represents about 38 percent of total official development assistance afforded by the developed to the developing countries.

Consequently, developing countries complain that the postwar changes in world economic activity, primarily determined by the interests of the major industrial nations, inflict substantial losses in foreign exchange earnings upon them and thereby retard their economic development. Taking into account the losses suffered by the oil-producing countries as a result of the main oil-importing countries' policy to maintain prices at

their 1950 level (a policy only recently readjusted
under extreme pressure), the drain imposed on the
Third World becomes even greater. If the oil prices
had been determined according to the index of world
prices, the exporting countries could have gained
several billions of dollars more in foreign exchange
and thus been able to finance plans for the faster
utilization of their material resources.

A further factor operating against the interests of developing countries is the steady decline
in the share of primary products in the composition
of international trade. Whereas in 1955 exports of
raw materials accounted for about 15 percent of
world exports, by 1968 the figure had dropped to
12.9 percent, while over the same period the value
of exported food and beverages declined from 20
percent to 14.5 percent.

These adverse trends in the foreign trade of
developing countries, associated primarily with a
poor export performance, are expected to cause a
steady increase in trade deficits. Moreover, acceleration of economic development is bound to ex-
pand imports of goods and services, and this will
further aggravate an already serious external imbalance.

The United Nations Council for Trade and Development (UNCTAD) undertook to estimate future
levels of exports, essential imports, and payments
for factor services (debt servicing and profits on
foreign investments) of developing countries for
the years 1975 and 1980, according to certain as-
sumptions about average annual growth rates for
each country during the 1970's. These projections
were submitted to the ninth session of UNCTAD (February, 1970) and are shown in Table 13.

According to the figures of Table 13, at an
assumed average annual growth rate of 6.1 percent
in GNP, the trade deficit of the developing nations
(exclusive of oil-producing countries) will rise to
$14.9 billion by 1975 and $26.7 billion by 1980.

TABLE 13

Projections of Trade Deficits of Developing Countries, 1975 and 1980
(in billions of U.S. dollars, 1960 prices)

	1963 (a)	1963 (b)	1975 (a)	1975 (b)	1980 (a)	1980 (b)
Exports						
Goods	31.8	24.3	65.2	43.0	92.4	51.0
Services	5.8	5.4	12.2	10.8	17.3	14.7
Total	37.6	29.7	77.4	53.8	109.7	65.7
Imports						
Goods	32.0	28.9	67.5	58.2	93.8	78.8
Services	5.5	4.4	13.0	10.5	18.0	13.6
Total	37.5	33.3	80.5	68.7	111.8	92.4
Trade balance	+0.1	-3.6	-3.1	-14.9	-2.1	-26.7
Current transfer payments factors (net)	-4.9	-2.3	-15.8	-7.5	-23.7	-10.8
Balance on current transactions	-4.8	-5.9	-18.9	-22.4	-25.8	-37.5

a All developing countries.
b Exclusive of oil-exporting countries.

Source: UNCTAD, Trade Projections for 1975 and 1980, Document TD/B26K revised by Document TD/B/264. Review No. 1 of December 30, 1969 (revised figures).

Inclusive of payments for debt servicing, the balance on current transactions (goods, services, and current transfers) for all developing countries (oil-exporting excluded) will show a deficit of $22.4 billion in 1975 and $37.5 billion in 1980. Therefore, it should be clear that the immediate prospects for the developing countries in their vital external sector are far from encouraging. This important issue will be further considered in Chapter 5.

THE POLICIES OF SPECIALIZED AGENCIES

Apart from the previously discussed factors that have a retarding effect on the economic development of the Third World, we must consider the policies pursued by several international specialized agencies. These policies are designed in principle to accelerate the development of this group of nations.

Origins of United Nations Efforts

The efforts of the United Nations to assist the development of low-income countries date back to the time of adoption of the United Nations Charter of San Francisco in 1945. A chapter of the Charter is devoted to international economic and social cooperation. It was then admitted that future generations could be saved from the scourge of war by abolishing the poverty and privation that make war possible. Thus, Article 55 of the Charter stipulates that, with a view to the creation of conditions of stability and well-being, the United Nations shall promote higher standards of living, full employment, and conditions of economic and social progress and development.

The first major effort in the field of international cooperation was the setting up of the United Nations Relief and Reconstruction Agency (UNRRA) in 1943. However, the main objective of UNRRA was not to provide development aid but to give relief and assist in the rehabilitation and reconstruction of

areas devastated by war. Moreover, the countries
assisted were almost exclusively developed countries of Western Europe. Subsequently, the Marshall
Plan was launched with similar objectives, although
the resources it made available were on a much larger scale. The United States, on the initiative of
General George Marshall, then Secretary of State,
operated a scheme to provide assistance to countries,
mainly in Europe, whose economies had been so seriously affected by World War II that their recovery
was likely to be slow. In 1948, the Organization
for European Economic Cooperation (OEEC) was established in connection with the Marshall Plan to administer United States aid to Europe. The volume
of resources provided through the Marshall Plan totaled $13 billion.*

Development aid proper originated in the resolutions of the United Nations General Assembly
(1946) and the Economic and Social Council and in
the declaration of U.S. President Harry S. Truman
in 1949, which resulted in "Point 4" and the Public
Law for International Development. However, the
motives behind these aid programs were not entirely
economic, but also "philanthropic and strategic."
On the whole, the programs were designed for reasons of political expediency.

However, in view of the extent to which former
colonial territories were acquiring political independence, world public opinion was becoming aware
of the magnitude of the requirements of low-income
countries and of the necessity to provide both substantial and continuous development aid. The first
important move toward meeting the developing countries' aid requirements was the establishment in
1949 of the extended Program of Technical Assistance,

---

*When this project was terminated, European
countries, together with the United States and
Canada, and Japan since 1964, jointly established
the Organization for Economic Cooperation and Development (OECD) whose objectives are of a more general importance.

initially designed to provide both experts and scholarships. This program subsequently was extended to assist developing countries in national planning and its implementation as an instrument for solving the crucial problems of their economic development, including those associated with accelerated industrialization. The Program of Technical Assistance is operated on the principle of political neutrality, and for that reason the United Nations adopted a resolution stipulating that the granting of technical assistance should entail no foreign intervention of an economic or political nature in the internal affairs of the recipient countries, nor should it have any political strings attached to it (Resolution 229 of the United Nations General Assembly, 1965).

The United Nations exercises its activities in the field of development through numerous international specialized agencies whose number is constantly increasing. There are already twelve specialized agencies affiliated with the United Nations, operating as intergovernmental separate autonomous organizations.* In addition, there are some dozens of semiautonomous bodies.**

---

*These twelve specialized agencies are: International Labor Organization (ILO), Food and Agriculture Organization (FAO), United Nations Educational, Scientific, and Cultural Organization (UNESCO), World Health Organization (WHO), International Civil Aviation Organization (ICAO), International Bank for Reconstruction and Development (IBRD), International Monetary Fund (IMF), Universal Postal Union (UPU), International Telecommunications Union (ITU), World Meteorological Organization (WMO), Inter-Governmental Maritime Consultative Organization (IMCO), and International Atomic Energy Agency (IAEA).

**Among the most important semiautonomous bodies one should mention: United Nations Conference on Trade and Development (UNCTAD), United Nations Industrial Development Organization (UNIDO), United

United Nations Development Program

The United Nations Development Program (UNDP)
is designed to operate as the main channel for multilateral technical and pre-investment assistance
to developing countries. These countries are helped
to create favorable conditions for mobilizing development capital on a sound and businesslike basis
from both domestic and external sources, and for
preparing the way for fully effective use of such
investment capital and all other available economic
and human assets.[4]

The main disadvantages of this type of development aid are its inadequate volume and the lack of
effective coordination. It should be recalled that
over the period 1959-69 voluntary contributions to
the Technical Assistance Program totaled $1,433 mil-
lion, while in 1969, the record year for financial
assistance to developing countries, the level of
aid reached only $200 million, a sum clearly inade-
quate in relation to the needs of these countries.
Moreover, these voluntary contributions come from
several specialized agencies (UN 25 percent, FAO
29 percent, UNESCO 14 percent, ILO 11 percent) and
many other organizations. Thus, total financial
contributions are divided in a manner that under-
mines their effective use.

United Nations Conference on
Trade and Development

The first United Nations Conference on Trade
and Development (UNCTAD) was convened in Geneva in
1964 and was entrusted with the study and preparation of recommendations on a number of issues of

---

Nations Development Program (UNDP), World Food Program (WFP), United Nations Institute for Training
and Research (UNITAR), and General Agreement on Tariffs and Trade (GATT), which, in certain respects,
are part of the United Nations system. By the end
of 1970, the United Nations bodies totaled 125.

direct importance to developing countries. The
recommendations of the first conference, which resulted in the establishment of UNCTAD as a permanent organ of the General Assembly in December,
1964, referred to the following subjects:

1. Removal of trade barriers and promotion
of international trade,
2. Arrangements for international trade in
primary products,
3. Expansion of trade among developing countries,
4. Problems associated with synthetic products
and substitutes for primary products.

Judged after a lapse of seven years, the results of these recommendations, which provoked pro-
longed discussion and heated argument by developing
nations, are admittedly limited. The admission of
failure comes from highly authoritative and competent sources. For instance, Raul Prebish, the driving force and Secretary General of UNCTAD until
1969, gave a highly pessimistic account of developments in his report to the second conference held
in February-March, 1968, in New Delhi. Here are
some of the points made in his report.[5]

Referring to the recommendations of the first
UNCTAD to remove barriers to international trade in
primary products, Mr. Prebish remarked that the
text of the recommendations contained so many reservations that barriers to trade had been maintained
and even extended. As regards competing products
exported by developing nations, industrialized countries, far from facilitating imports of such goods,
were seeking to exclude them from their markets by
means of fiscal imposts. The recent imposition of
a 10 percent surcharge by President Nixon is a
further measure expected to aggravate an already
serious situation.

As regards the UNCTAD recommendation that importing countries that impose internal taxes on primary products should reimburse supplying developing

nations with part of the revenue from these taxes, Mr. Prebish remarked that "so far it has not induced importing countries to do so." Similarly disappointing are the results from the recommendations to set up international schemes for stabilizing primary product prices. In the words of Mr. Prebish, "Two years of discussions have not yet produced an agreement on cocoa."

Lastly, on the important, novel, and controversial proposal for the establishment of preferences in the markets of developed countries for exports of manufactures and semimanufactures by the developing countries, Mr. Prebish noted that, although the idea had gained a great deal of ground, "important points still remain to be clarified."

Another proposal related to the promotion of trade and economic integration among developing countries. Although this proposal commanded a large measure of acceptance by all interested countries, in practice no concrete policy measures have been formulated.

Lastly, mention should be made of the problem of quantitative restrictions on certain exports by developing countries; these restrictions belong to the group of nontariff barriers to trade.

EVALUATION OF UNITED NATIONS POLICY

At this point, several crucial issues must be referred to. They arise out of the fact that virtually none of the recommendations of the first UNCTAD were ever implemented.

Who shares the blame for this failure: the developing countries alone or UNCTAD for making unrealistic recommendations that proved difficult to implement, or for underestimating the significance of certain crucial factors in the process of development?

It is our belief that the first UNCTAD was misguided on the issue of priorities to be established
within the overall development strategy. In fact,
one cannot help being surprised at the lack of real-
ism apparent in a number of UNCTAD recommendations
and in a series of international arrangements resulting therefrom. For instance, to demand international arrangements for the stabilization of primary product prices is neither practical nor beneficial to the developing countries. The object of
UNCTAD was to combine export restriction schemes
with the operation of a mechanism of buffer stocks
designed to absorb surpluses of certain commodities
in years of excessive output and to market them
when production subsequently fell below the level
of world demand. The ultimate objective of this
scheme was to contain price fluctuations within
fixed limits. The scheme was to have been applied
to cocoa, sugar, tea, coffee, wheat, rubber, and
copper.

Even a limited price stabilization could prove
advantageous to developing nations, provided it
could be extended to include not only their primary
products but also manufactured and semimanufactured
goods of the developed countries. This broadening
of scope is rightly considered an indispensable com-
plementary measure since the attempt to stabilize
prices of primary products only, without the possibility of upward adjustment necessitated by persistent inflation, would be detrimental to the legitimate interests of developing nations. They have
very little to gain from limiting the upward move-
ment of prices of their exportable products. On
the other hand, their prime interest lies in preventing a sudden fall in prices, since this means a
real loss in foreign exchange earnings. The proposed mechanism is not an adequate means of achieving the desired objective. An effective price stabilization scheme should equally operate, according
to a plan of general compensatory financing, in
cases of a sudden decline in world prices.

Moreover, price fluctuations are determined by changes in domestic output and world demand, by weather conditions affecting the volume of almost all primary products, and by technological developments in the field of synthetic substitutes. Whereas in the past from time to time prices of certain primary products slumped quite appreciably, over the last few years prices have shown a significant rise that has improved the foreign exchange earning capacity of the exporting countries. Thus, in 1968, for the third consecutive year, the price of cocoa went up 16 percent, while the price of rice rose approximately 10 percent above the 1967 level. Copper prices remained unchanged in 1968 after rising by 17 percent between 1963 and 1968. In the course of 1969 there was a sharp increase in coffee prices. In comparison with 1963 the price of copper in 1967 had risen by 52 percent, while jute prices went up 18 percent over the same period. In the case of other primary products, such as tea, wool, and cotton, a slight drop in prices took place, although on the whole prices of these products have remained at the high 1967 world level.[6]

The difficulties inherent in the conclusion of an international agreement on any primary product are enormous, and consequently such international schemes are mostly doomed to failure.[7]

Gains and Losses

A closer analysis of developments during the 1965-67 period reveals that developing countries made profits on their exports but sustained heavy losses on their imports. Table 14 shows the balance of gains and losses in three selected years.

These figures show that over the period 1965-67 developing countries suffered an aggregate loss in foreign exchange earnings of $1.3 billion as a result of the adverse movement in their terms of trade with developed countries. This significant drain is exclusively attributable to the faster rise in the prices paid by the developing countries

for their imported commodities and the slower rate
of increase in the prices obtained for their exports.
Consequently, in the event of the adoption of a
scheme for stabilizing export prices, developing nations would have sustained an additional loss of
$258 million, since they are in no position to pre-
vent rises in import prices.

Under such conditions, it is very doubtful
whether a scheme for the stabilization of primary
product prices can serve any useful purpose unless
there is simultaneous stabilization of the prices of
manufactures and semimanufactures produced by developed countries. Such a proposal would be meaningful
if it were aimed at effecting an alignment of primary
product prices, as is the case with the recent Tripoli
agreement on oil prices. This arrangement would ensure an equilibrium between the price levels of primary products and manufactures. However, there are
serious doubts as to the feasibility of such an international commodity arrangement.

TABLE 14

Balance of Gains and Losses of Developing
Countries, 1965-67
(millions of U.S. dollars)

Year	Gains Through Exports	Losses Through Imports	Total Balance
1965	156	1,038	-882
1966	442	1,407	-965
1967	175	2,243	-2,068
Annual average	258	1,563	-1,305

Source: United Nations, Survey of International Trade and Development, 1969 (New York, 1969),
Table 23.

The preoccupation of the first and second
UNCTAD with issues inherently difficult to solve
resulted in weakening, and relegating to second
place, policy measures of the first importance for
the progress of developing nations.[8] It is odd
that UNCTAD insists on this approach despite the
meager results in the field of primary products
agreements, as can be seen in its draft report for
the second Development Decade. This document again
emphasizes that the highest priority should be assigned to efforts aimed at securing stable, remuner-
ative, and equitable prices for primary products,
with the problem of financing relegated to second
place. As regards the central issue of development
financing, the UNCTAD document recommends that developed countries consider measures designed to ease
the terms of aid still further and adds that it is
the developing countries that must and in fact do
carry the major burden of the financing of their
own development.[9]

The UNCTAD report makes only a vague reference
to the subject of excessive indebtedness of the
Third World, as though it attaches minor importance
to this crucial problem. The progress of the developing nations will be determined by two factors:
(1) financing on favorable terms and (2) trade preferences for the exports of their manufactures and
semimanufactures to the markets of the developed
countries. A certain measure of progress has been
made as regards the second of these factors. However, the problem of easier development aid has yet
to be resolutely tackled; in our opinion this problem should be the overriding priority for the Third
World countries.

The "Most Complex Machinery in the World"

Although the United Nations has made praiseworthy efforts in the field of social and economic
development and has rendered signal service in
placing the question of progress of the developing
nations in the forefront of world problems, results
have not been commensurate with expectations. In

fact, the existence of numerous specialized agencies, often overlapping in their terms of reference, the lack of effective coordination of activities, a complex and not easily manageable bureaucracy, a succession of conferences that fail to produce realistic plans for action--all this goes with a world policy that is highly controversial and very costly[10] while for the most part its results are out of proportion to the financial resources deployed.

We are not alone in this critical view of United Nations activities. Highly qualified persons within the organization itself deplore the present state of affairs. Thus, in his annual report on the work of the United Nations (June 16, 1967-June 15, 1968), Secretary General U Thant observed that

> the achievements of the second session of UNCTAD held in 1968 at New Delhi were very limited. Its proceedings and decisions suggest that the political will to work towards concerted action was lacking. The negotiations, in the broad sense of the term, were not conducted with the desire to arrive at results; the constructive spirit, the required steadfastness of purpose, and the will for action were lost in the labyrinth of a cumbersome and inadequate institutional mechanism.

In concluding his annual report the Secretary General remarked, "It is particularly regrettable that the Conference was thus unable to make any significant contribution towards the formulation of a global strategy for development."[11]

More bitter criticism of the method of operation of the United Nations and its specialized agencies can be found in the report of M. Jackson, President of the Commission for the study of the Development Capacity of the United Nations System.[12] In this appraisal of the experience of UN activities

in general, and in the field of development in particular, during the first 25 years, concern is expressed at the great inertia of the United Nations'
elaborate administrative structure, which no one
can change although change is now imperative. According to the aforesaid study, the United Nations
machine has grown over the decades into what is
probably the most complex organization in the world.

> In theory it is under the control of
> about thirty separate governing bodies;
> in the past, much of their work in deal-
> ing with administrative problems has
> been self-defeating. At the headquar-
> ters level there is no real "headpiece"--
> no central co-ordinating organization--
> which could exercise effective control.
> Below that level, the administrative
> tentacles thrust downwards into an ex-
> traordinary complex of regional and
> sub-regional offices, and finally ex-
> tend into field offices in over ninety
> developing countries. This "Machine"
> now has a marked identity of its own
> and its power is so great that the
> question must be asked, "Who controls
> this 'Machine'?" So far, the evi-
> dence suggests that governments do not,
> and also that the machine is incapable
> of intelligently controlling itself.
> This is not because it lacks intelli-
> gent and capable officials, but be-
> cause it is so organized that mana-
> gerial direction is impossible. In
> other words, the machine as a whole
> has become unmanageable in the
> strictest use of the word. As a re-
> sult, it is becoming slower and more
> unwieldy, like some prehistoric mon-
> ster.[13]

Two years have passed since the publication
of Jackson's report, and nothing has been done to
implement its constructive proposals for a more

effective coordination of the United Nations development programs.

The results achieved during the first 25 years through the activities of the United Nations and its specialized agencies in the field of social and economic development have not come up to the expectations of those who believed that satisfactory solutions could be found for the problems of economic backwardness. A revision of administrative structures and methods of operation is essential if the United Nations and the specialized agencies are to become capable of undertaking such vigorous and concerted action as will make possible the solution of the difficulties of the developing countries and will assist them in the task of accelerating their socioeconomic progress.

NOTES

1. According to a study by the Indian economist B. R. Shenoy, "significant portions of economic aid were lost because of waste and squandering, both internal and external." Among external causes of wasteful use, the author includes financing of gold smuggling and luxury goods, illegal exports of capital, etc. The 1968-69 value of contraband trade alone totaled $373 million on an aggregate value of $1,030 million in aid provided during the same period. Consequently, squandering of foreign resources through contraband amounted to as much as 36 percent of total external aid. See Far Eastern Economic Review, August 27, 1970.

2. See Statistical Office of the United Nations, Yearbook of International Trade Statistics, Supplement 1970 (New York, 1970, Sales No. 70.XVII.11), pp. 2, 4.

3. See Review of International Trade and Development, 1967 (New York, 1968, Sales No. E.68. II.D.4).

4. Details about the activities of the United Nations Development Program (UNDP) can be found in External Financing of Economic Development: International Flow of Long-Term Capital and Official Donations, 1970 (New York: United Nations, 1970, Sales No. E.70.II.A.3) and in the 1969 report of UNDP Director General, Paul Hoffmann.

5. See International Development Strategy for 1970's (New York: United Nations, 1968, Sales No. F.68.II.D.6).

6. The figures cited are taken from Review of Recent Trends in Trade and Development, 1969 (New York: United Nations, 1970, Sales No. E.70.II.D.4).

7. This inability of the international community to help was admitted by the Pearson Commission in the following statement: "Several primary products do not seem to require any special international action. And even within the field of 'problem commodities' there are enormous differences in the conditions of production and demand, and in the characteristics of different commodities. Thus, no single prescription is likely to solve their divergent problems." See Partners in Development: Report of the Commission on International Development (New York: Praeger Publishers, 1969), p. 81. Moreover, the United Nations Conference on Wheat, convened for about five weeks in Geneva in February, 1971, failed to conclude a new agreement fixing maximum and minimum prices for the world market of wheat.

8. See Review of Recent Trends in Trade and Development, 1969, op. cit., p. 24.

9. Jacques L'Huillier who, in a highly interesting study, appraises the policy of UNCTAD on primary products, expresses great skepticism about the success of such measures. He draws the conclusion that the proposals aimed at accelerating development rates by direct intervention on the export earnings of primary products create the impression of deception. Moreover, he cannot refrain

from remarking that "in order to justify the persistent search for a solution from the point of view
of primary products one invokes a realistic argument: one should start from the product which de-
serves to exist. However, such an argument could
legitimize all these rigidities." See Les Organi-
sations internationales de coopération économique
et le commerce extérieur des pays en voie de développement (Geneva: Institut Universitaire de Genève,
1969), p. 45. See UNCTAD and the Second United Nations Development Decade (New York: United Nations,
January, 1970, Document TD/B/L/206), p. 17.

    10. The regular budget of the specialized
agencies of the United Nations (not including the
Bank Group, IMF, and GATT) almost tripled between
1960 and 1969 and is distributed as follows (in
millions of U.S. dollars):

Specialized Agency		1960	1969
FAO		10.6	33.6
UNESCO		13.8	42.1
WHO		17.1	67.4
ILO		9.6	31.1
IAEA		5.2	12.6
WMO		0.6	3.2
ITU		2.3	7.5
UPU		0.6	2.0
ICAO		4.6	8.0
IMCO		0.3	1.1
	Total	64.8	208.7
UN including UNCTAD and UNIDO		65.8	151.2
	Total	130.6	359.9
Voluntary Contribu- tions to Expanded Program of Technical Assistance (EPTA), Special Fund, and UNDP		72.6	197.4
	Grand Total	203.2	557.3

See A Study of the Capacity of the United Nations
Development System (Geneva: United Nations, 1969,
Sales No. E.70.I.10), Vol. II, Appendix Six,
Table 4.

11.   See A/7201/Supplement I.   September 24, 1968, p. 11.

12.   See <u>A Study of the Capacity of the United Nations Development System</u>, <u>op. cit.</u>, Vols. I-II.

13.   <u>Ibid.</u>, Vol. I, pp. II-III.

4

THE MYTH
OF DEVELOPMENT
AID

THE NEED FOR REAL AID

For all countries, economic development is primarily a national responsibility. It is of particular concern to developing countries that are desirous of raising the extremely low living standards of their populations. To this end, and taking into account the progress of the present technological revolution, these countries draw up and implement long-term development plans designed to mobilize their unutilized material and human resources, to assure full employment for the part of their active population that at present is suffering from unemployment and underemployment, and to accelerate socioeconomic progress in general.

The success of these development plans depends largely on the existence of a favorable climate of international cooperation and on an adequate flow of financial aid from the industrialized to the developing countries, especially during the initial stages of the development effort. However, the efficacy of this aid will depend primarily on the nature and magnitude of the efforts of the aid-receiving countries themselves. A conjunction of

these two factors--national effort and international
cooperation--is a precondition of a satisfactory
solution of the problem of underdevelopment. In a
vicious circle of cause and effect, underdevelopment itself constitutes the major obstacle to development.

Experience has amply shown that economically
backward countries tend to stagnate in a state of
self-perpetuating poverty that prevents them from
breaking out of this vicious circle and setting out
along the road to rapid and self-sustained growth.
As we have already noted, this poverty results in
low productivity, per capita incomes that are too
low to permit savings adequate to finance the
amount of investment that is indispensable for the
utilization of idle national resources.

ACCENTUATION OF STRUCTURAL IMBALANCES

Technological progress tends to complicate the
situation still further. Despite their vast potentialities, technological advances tend to aggravate
existing obstacles to socioeconomic development by
accentuating the persistent tendency toward structural disequilibrium, particularly in the balance
of trade, and by widening the gap between domestic
saving and investment.

The adoption of technological innovations in
industrial development and in the mechanization of
agriculture requires a growing volume of investment,
which cannot be financed out of the low volume of
domestic saving. Moreover, the advances in science
and technology result in a sharp decline in mortality rates and an increase in life expectancy, and
ultimately limit the capacity to save. Thus, the
volume of domestic savings that can be channeled
into productive investment to accelerate economic
development decreases. The significance of this
savings/investment problem can be seen in the fact
that population growth in developing countries
reaches such a high rate that two-thirds of

aggregate investment must be devoted to meeting the requirements of the additional population, whereas in the developed countries this ratio never exceeds one-fourth.

Technological progress also tends to have an unbalancing impact on the external sector by adversely affecting exports of primary products, which also suffer from the effects of price fluctuations. Furthermore, improvement in living standards tends to induce an expansion in imports of foreign goods. The combined effect of these imbalances is to slow down growth rates, unless foreign resources are made available to bridge the savings and foreign exchange gaps.[1]

However, foreign aid to developing countries is not required exclusively to supplement pivotal scarcities of material resources. Its most constructive use is to improve the provision of professional training, to introduce new techniques and innovations, to develop new and more efficient methods of management, and to improve general educational standards. Technical assistance clearly must play a vital role in this area of development. For the accelerated utilization of domestic material and human resources, it is essential to make available experts, consultants, engineers, and specialist advisers for the preparation and launching of technical projects.

Finally, the psychological role of external development assistance must not be underestimated. The inflow of foreign financial resources in conjunction with advanced "know-how" creates, in the recipient countries, a climate of opinion that will back national governments in the adoption of imaginative and vigorous policies.

International cooperation is thus indispensable for overcoming the major obstacles to socioeconomic progress and for accelerating growth rates. In this context, the stand taken against development assistance by P. T. Bauer of the London School of

Economics is in conflict with reality. Moreover, his assertion that Europe developed without outside aid has no relevance to the Third World of today.[2] It should not be forgotten that during its development phase Europe was the leading industrial region of the world, and that subsequently Europe even provided assistance that made possible the rapid development of the U.S. economy.

However, international aid to developing countries should not be of a permanent nature. It is essential during the take-off stage of a country's economy to make possible the acceleration of development up to the point at which the country can maintain a satisfactory rate of growth by its own resources. Therefore, the external aid should be only temporary. Furthermore, the aid should be given as such, namely, in the form of grants and/or grant-like contributions or, at the least, on extremely favorable terms. Under any other form, it is no longer aid in the proper sense of the term but a normal type of financing, often provided on terms that hamper rather than assist economic development.

THE VOLUME AND PATTERN OF DEVELOPMENT AID

During the 1960's, foreign aid assumed a more definite form. As the developing nations sucessively became members of the United Nations, the urgent problem of the low living standards of their populations was increasingly brought to the attention of the General Assembly. Furthermore, several specialized agencies were established to deal with particular aspects of social and economic development. One of these agencies was UNCTAD, which was established as a permanent organ of the General Assembly in December, 1964. Another was the United Nations Industrial Development Organization (UNIDO), set up on January 1, 1967, to promote industrial development and help accelerate the industrialization of developing countries.

However, the organization specifically designed to provide development assistance is the Development Assistance Committee (DAC), known at
first as the Development Assistance Group.* DAC
was created in 1961 as an affiliated agency of OECD
to provide a needed meeting place where suppliers
of bilateral assistance to developing countries
could consult and exchange experience on common
problems. Its initial concern was with the equitable sharing of the responsibility for providing assistance. However, its interest in the volume of
assistance quickly extended to other related questions, as can be judged from the number of recommendations included in its annual reports on development assistance.

The Pattern of Development Assistance

In Table 15 the financial resources provided
by industrialized countries (members of DAC) to developing nations and to multilateral agencies are
broken down into the following three groups:

1. Official development assistance, consisting of grants, grant-like contributions, and other
soft loans;

2. Other official assistance, including public suppliers' credits, official multilateral assistance, net (grants and capital subscriptions),
bonds, loans, and participations in multilateral
agencies;

----

*The members of the Development Assistance Com-
mittee (DAC) are Australia, Austria, Belgium, Canada, Denmark, France, West Germany, Italy, Japan,
Netherlands, Norway, Portugal, Sweden, Switzerland,
United Kingdom, United States, and the Commission
of European Communities. The IBRD and IMF participate in the work of DAC in the capacity of observ-
ers.

TABLE 15

Flow of Long-Term Financial Resources from DAC Countries, 1960-70

(millions of U.S. dollars)

Disbursements, Net	1960	1965	1969	1970
Total official and private	8,115	10,413	13,297	14,712
1. Official development assistance	4,703	5,936	6,682	6,813
a. Bilateral grants	3,716	3,770	3,350	3,298
b. Bilateral loans	452	1,723	2,302	2,400
c. Contributions to multilateral agencies	535	443	1,030	1,115
2. Other official assistance	262	302	566	1,135
a. Bilateral	195	297	575	864
b. Multilateral	67	5	9	271
3. Private investment and lending	3,150	4,174	6,047	6,764
a. Direct investment	1,767	2,489	2,566	3,412
b. Bilateral portfolio investment	633	687	1,334	837
c. Multilateral portfolio investment	204	248	413	343
d. Export credits	546	750	1,734	2,172
Total official and private (1 + 2)	4,965	6,238	7,248	7,948

Source: The figures referred to in this study on the volume of development assistance were taken from the OECD publications Development Assistance Efforts and Policies 1968, 1969 and 1970 Review, and other United Nations publications, among which one should mention External Financing of Economic Development: International Flow of Long-term Capital and Official Donations 1964-1968 (New York: United Nations, 1970). According to the OECD press release (June 20, 1971) containing the provisional figures for the 1970 volume of development assistance, total official and private flow to less developed countries and multilateral agencies reached the $15,552 million level instead of $14,712 million mentioned herein. The difference of $840 million represents "private grants for development purposes by private voluntary agencies," of which $578 million were provided by the United States. However, for the sake of a comparative study this item is excluded because for previous years no statistically reliable figures existed, according to the aforesaid press release. These "grants" are defined as expenses for development assistance and grants for development purposes provided by private voluntary non-profit agencies.

3. Private flow, consisting of private investment (direct and portfolio), private lending,
and private export credits for over one year.

Table 15 shows the net flow of long-term financial resources* to developing countries and
multilateral agencies over the years 1960-70.

According to the statistics in Table 15, the
aggregate flow of financial resources from the DAC
member countries to developing nations and multilateral agencies during the 1960's increased in
absolute figures. Thus, development assistance
rose from $8.1 billion in 1960 to $10.4 billion in
1965 and $14.7 billion in 1970.

During the same decade, the flow of development assistance from the centrally planned economies (communist countries) to developing countries
did not exceed the level of $300 to $350 million
annually.[3] Moreover, the volume of aid provided by
the U.S.S.R. and the other countries of the Eastern
bloc to developing communist nations was of the
order of $9.8 billion for the period 1947-68.**
According to a recent review of communist aid, net
flows from the communist countries ebbed from the
mid-1960's to the end of the decade. Although new
aid offered in 1970 showed an increase for the second year in succession and the total of $1,160 mil-
lion exceeded the average of the 1964-68 period (of
$1,000 million per year), it was still below the
peak year of 1964 when $1,700 million was offered.
The 1970 total included the massive Chinese credits
of $400 million for the building of the Zambia-
Tanzania railroad; this represents the largest

---

*Net flow of financial resources equals gross
flow minus amortization received on previous loans.

**The beneficiaries of this aid were the Peo-
ple's Republic of China to the amount of $3.5 bil-
lion, Cuba $3.2 billion, and North Vietnam $3.1
billion.

single lump of aid given by the communist countries
for any project, even bigger than the $325 million
from the Soviet Union for the Aswan High Dam. It
is significant that China made a major comeback to
the aid field with a total of $695 million in 1970,
making it by far the largest donor in the communist
area.

A Target for Development Assistance

Is the flow of financial aid from the industrialized countries, totaling $14.7 billion in 1970
and $102.5 billion during the 1960's, really ade-
quate and in conformity with the recommendations
made by the international organizations? This is
an important question requiring closer examination.

The question of the volume of development assistance has been discussed at various international conferences in relation to the problem of underdevelopment. As early as 1960, the United Nations
General Assembly adopted a resolution expressing
the hope that the flow of assistance and international capital would be increased appreciably in
order to attain, as early as possible, the target
of 1 percent of the combined GNP of the economically advanced countries. This recommendation was
formulated in a more concrete form at the first
UNCTAD in 1964, when it was decided that the 1 percent target did not refer to "the economically advanced countries taken as a whole," as the United
Nations General Assembly had suggested, but to each
individual country.

At the second UNCTAD, held in New Delhi in
February-March, 1968, a key decision was the recommendation that each economically advanced country
should strive to provide the developing nations
with an annual transfer of financial resources to
the extent of not less than 1 percent of its GNP at
market prices, rather than 1 percent of its national income.[4] This would give a 25 percent increase
over the initial target. Lastly, DAC reaffirmed in
1968 the intention of its member countries to do

their utmost to attain the new target of 1 percent
of their GNP.

THE PROGRESSIVE FALL IN AID AS
A PERCENTAGE OF GNP

Although the aggregate financial resources
provided by the economically advanced countries to
developing nations showed an increase in absolute
figures for the period 1960-69, their development
assistance as a percentage of GNP showed a steady
decline. Whereas in 1961, for the DAC group as a
whole, the flow of net official and private dis-
bursements was 0.96 percent of the combined GNP,
this ratio dropped to 0.79 percent in 1968 and 0.74
percent in 1970. This trend is shown in Table 16.
The decline was more pronounced in the sector of
official assistance, where the ratio to GNP dropped
from 0.54 percent to 0.36 percent between 1961 and
1969.

As against the steady decline in the official
flow of financial resources to developing nations,
which up to 1965 accounted for almost half the combined development assistance of the DAC countries,
the flow of private long-term financial resources
over the same number of years shows a clear upward
trend and almost doubled between 1964 ($3.2 bil-
lion) and 1969 ($6.8 billion). The major part of
private flows (about two-thirds) consists of direct
investment which, together with portfolio investment (bilateral and multilateral), totaled $4.1
billion in 1970. Private export credits, another
type of private flow of financial resources, have
tripled in the last few years and totaled $2 bil-
lion in 1970. However, this flow of private export
credits (commercial credits granted mainly by West
Germany, Japan, France, and the United Kingdom)
represents a type of financing provided on unfavorable terms, namely for short periods and at high
interest rates. This sharp rise in the volume of
private export credits creates serious problems for
the developing countries since the growing reliance

TABLE 16

Flow of Long-Term Financial Resources from
Total DAC Countries by Major Group and
Expressed as Percentages of GNP
(billions of U.S. dollars)

	1960	1961	1968	1970
Total official and private flows, net	8.1	9.2	13.2	14.7
Percentage of GNP	0.89	0.96	0.79	0.74
Official development assistance	4.7	5.2	6.4	6.8
Percentage of GNP	0.52	0.54	0.38	0.34
Total official multi- lateral development assistance	0.5	0.5	0.7	1.1
Percentage of GNP	0.05	0.05	0.04	0.06

Note: GNP at market prices.

Source: DAC Report, 1971.

on this type of financing tends to aggravate
balance-of-payments difficulties. Argentina, Brazil, Chile, and certain other countries already are
overindebted in respect of export credits and sooner or later will be compelled to seek a radical revision of their foreign debt obligations.

The Sharp Fall in U.S. Development Aid

An analysis of the volume of financial resources provided by the economically advanced countries leads to disappointing conclusions. The
United States, the world's richest country, had
been supplying about half the total of official

flows of financial resources to developing countries. Since 1969, however, the U.S. contribution
has dropped both in absolute terms and as a percentage of GNP: it fell from 0.66 percent of GNP
in 1968 to 0.49 percent in 1969 and only 0.30 percent in 1970. The largest fall occurred in the
sector of official long-term financial resources,
where the total dropped from $4.6 billion to $3.1
billion in 1969 and $1.8 billion in 1970. More-
over, over a quarter of the 1970 total of $1.8 bil-
lion--about $500 million--was channeled to southeast
Asia primarily for political reasons and thus hardly qualifies as "development assistance."* These
recent changes are all the more striking as in
1949, at the initial stage of the Marshall Plan,
American economic assistance amounted to as much as
2.70 percent of the U.S. GNP and 11.5 percent of
federal budget expenditure, whereas in 1970 the respective ratios were only 0.3 percent and less than
1 percent.[5]

In April, 1971, President Richard Nixon submitted to Congress a proposal for radical revision
of the various foreign aid programs by strict sepa-
ration of military assistance programs from economic
and humanitarian aid. Under this proposal, total
credits for the fiscal year 1971-72 will amount to
$3.3 billion, made up of $2 billion in military assistance and $1.3 billion in economic aid. Thus,
assuming Congressional approval of the plan, U.S.
development assistance to the developing countries
will reach its lowest level ever and will amount to
barely 0.13 percent of the U.S. GNP. This decline
in the U.S. contribution in financial resources

---

*The same comment applies to such countries as
the United Kingdom, France, and Portugal which provide military aid as part of the development assistance. It should be noted that Portugal, which
up to 1968 rated first in terms of aid as percentage of GNP, devoted substantial sums for the maintenance of troops in Angola, Mozambique, and Guinea.

lowers the overall percentage of DAC development
assistance. The situation became even more serious
following the decision of the American government
in August, 1971 to cut all foreign aid by 10 percent, and especially after the decision of the Sen-
ate to limit foreign aid and put in doubt its whole
structure. All indications point to the fact that
a new era has begun in the field of American foreign aid, which totaled nearly $150 billion during
the years 1945-70. The distribution of this amount
containing economic and military aid, according to
the Agency for International Development (AID), is
shown in Table 17.

TABLE 17

Distribution of U.S. Foreign Aid, 1945-70

Region and Country	Millions of U.S. Dollars
Europe	49,343
Britain	9,694
France	9,603
Italy	6,442
West Germany	5,089
Turkey	5,974
Greece	3,994
Yugoslavia	2,927
Far East	34,610
Near East and South Asia	31,984
Western Hemisphere	17,101
Africa	5,355
Oceania	1,588
Total U.S. foreign aid	149,585

Six Countries that Give Aid
Exceeding the Target

In 1970, six of the 15 DAC member countries--
Belgium, Denmark, France, West Germany, Italy, and
the Netherlands--provided financial resources ex-
ceeding 1 percent of their GNP. Three other countries have expressed their intention to equal this
performance in the near future: Sweden by 1972,
Norway by 1974, and Japan by 1975. Switzerland had
already exceeded the 1 percent target in 1968 when
its contribution amounted to 1.41 percent of GNP,
but the figure fell back to 0.66 percent in 1970 as
a result of a sharp fall in the flow of private financial resources. France's contribution dropped
from 1.36 percent in 1968 to 1.24 percent in 1970.
As a result of certain structural reforms in the
administration of development assistance and cuts
in the credits earmarked for cultural cooperation
and technical assistance contributions, there has
since been a further decline in the ratio of aid to
GNP, although it is still above 1 percent.

Since 1965, both West Germany and Japan have
appreciably increased their contributions, which
for 1969 amounted to 1.30 percent and 0.78 percent
of the GNP of West Germany and Japan, respectively.
Moreover, these two countries, which together with
France and the United Kingdom account for 31 percent
of the GNP of Western industrial countries, supplied in 1969 as much as 45 percent of DAC's total
net flows of financial resources. By contrast, the
United States, which accounts for 52 percent of the
combined GNP of DAC members, provided only 35 percent of total development assistance in 1969, and
this proportion dropped to about 25 percent in 1970
and declined still further during 1971.

As already stated, the greater part of the
contribution made by these countries comes from the
private sector and therefore represents normal financing on strictly commercial terms, while the official aid flows do not exceed 0.40 percent of GNP.
For 1969, the ratio of official flows of financial

resources to GNP was 0.39 percent for West Germany
and the United Kingdom, and 0.26 percent for Japan,
while for France the ratio was 0.69 percent, or almost at the 0.70 percent level recommended by the
United Nations.

Inequalities in Allocation of Development Assistance

The inadequacy of the amount of development
assistance appears even more striking when its geographical distribution is examined. Thus, half of
the official assistance goes to Asia, one-quarter
to Africa, and about 15 percent to Latin America.
The remaining 11 percent is allocated to certain
countries of Western Europe and Oceania. Aid received annually, expressed in dollars per capita of
the population, works out at an insignificant
amount. Asia ranks last with $2.73 per capita,
Latin America occupies a middle place with $3.30,
while Africa heads the list with $5.26. The pat-
tern of allocation shows very wide differences from
country to country within the same region. Thus,
in 1965 official development assistance worked out
to $32.8 per capita for Liberia, $1.2 for Ethiopia,
and $59 for Israel, while Indonesia received per
capita aid of only $0.40 and Argentina's share was
negligible.

These large differences in the geographical
distribution of official aid are the result of complex considerations mainly determined by historical
and political links (e.g., former colonies) existing between aid-supplying and aid-receiving countries. To redress this inequality in the allocation of development assistance, DAC proposed a new
system: that each country should receive a minimum
amount of aid irrespective of the size of the population and a further amount proportionate to its
population. Under this dual method of allocation,
during the period 1964-67 each assisted country
would have received a minimum of $18.6 million of
aid per annum plus an additional $2.30 per inhabi-
tant.

However, even this proposal to adjust the inadequate and therefore ineffectual pattern of aid
allocation was not endorsed by all donor countries.
One must draw the obvious conclusion that the system of bilateral aid agreements does not serve the
interests of developing countries and that therefore a politically neutral international agency is
required to bring about a more equitable distribution of development assistance.

Actual Development Aid in Comparison
to the Target

The preceding analysis shows that not only
have the economically advanced countries of the
West as a whole failed to attain even the 1 percent
of GNP objective but that their contribution of financial resources has been steadily declining and
falls short of the 1960-62 level by as much as 27
percent. Moreover, instead of an aggregate amount
of $18.4 billion that would have corresponded to
the 1 percent of GNP target, developing countries
received only $13.3 billion in aid, or $5.1 billion
short (the combined GNP at market prices for the
DAC member countries totaled $1,842 billion in
1969). If the system of 1 percent of GNP had been
observed during the six-year period 1963-69, the
developing countries would have received $30 bil-
lion more than they actually did (from the 1960-62
period to 1969, the GNP of DAC member countries
went up 88 percent whereas development assistance
during the same period rose only 54 percent). It
is estimated that to reach the target of 1 percent
of their combined GNP by 1975, DAC members would
have to contribute a net amount of about $21 bil-
lion of financial resources, both official and private (see Figure 6).

THE SMALL PROPORTION OF GRANTS
IN DEVELOPMENT AID

We now turn to another crucial aspect of the
problem of effective development assistance. When

speaking of assistance or aid made available by the
rich to the poor countries, one is generally inclined to assume that it is provided on a free or
grant basis. Whenever satisfaction is expressed at
the United Nations recommendation that economically
advanced countries annually devote 1 percent of
their GNP to accelerating the social and economic
progress of developing nations, world public opinion assumes that it is a question of providing
genuinely free aid in accordance with the lofty
ideal of international solidarity.

This assumption is quite false since, out of
an aggregate flow of $13.3 billion in development
assistance in 1969, only $4.4 billion or about 33
percent was in the form of grants and grant-like
contributions. The balance consisted of loans on
normal commercial terms, often at high interest
rates and, in most cases, with the stipulation of
short-term repayment of the principal. In other
words, it is a question of a normal system of financing whose terms sometimes prove more onerous
than those accorded to developed countries in respect of their borrowings from the world money markets. Figure 6 outlines the evolution of total financial flows during the 1960's and their make-up
in grants and loans. As shown by Figure 7, the
volume of "grants"[6] dropped appreciably between the
three-year period 1960-62 and the year 1969, namely
from 51.9 percent to 32.9 percent of the aggregate
flow of financial resources. Moreover, the ratio
of "grants" to total official flows declined from
an average of 80 percent for the period 1960-62 to
60 percent for 1969. The downward trend still persists and will probably become more marked in the
course of the early 1970's.

One of the factors responsible for this fall
is the progressive reduction in U.S. loans repayable in the currencies of the recipient countries.
These loans were included in the group of grant-
like contributions that were to be entirely discon-
tinued by the end of 1971. Consequently, despite
the substantial growth in contributions to

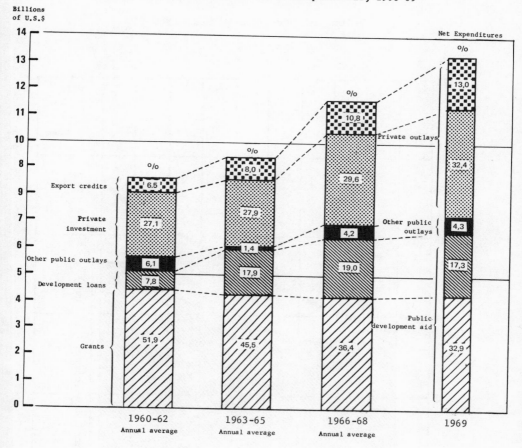

FIGURE 6

Structure of Total Flows of Development Aid, 1960-69

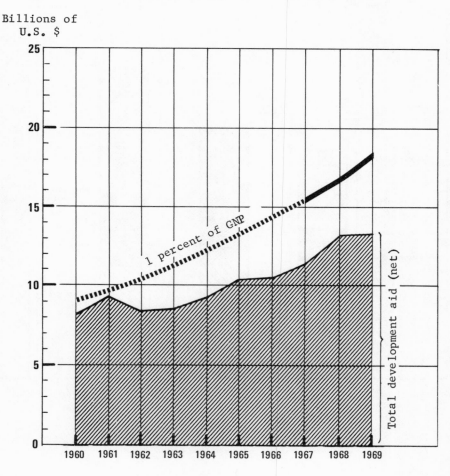

FIGURE 7

Volume of Development Aid, 1960-69

multilateral agencies since 1965, the "gift" element in the total volume of official flows of financial resources has diminished and there are no
indications of any reversal of this trend in the
near future.

In these circumstances, one wonders why international agencies, and in particular DAC, whose efforts to improve the term of financing of developing countries are praiseworthy, include private investment and lending under the heading of "development assistance." In this context, it would be
more correct to refer to official flows of $6.8
billion only as development aid for 1970, instead
of putting under this heading the amount of $14.7
billion, namely the grand total of official and
private flows. Of this aggregate flow of financial
resources to developing countries, the "gift" element accounts for only 50 percent.

The Difference Between Grants and Gifts

Moreover, the percentage share of grants and
grant-like contributions is not equivalent to aid
supplied entirely gratis. In practice, the term
"grant" as used by specialized agencies has a con-
notation different from that attached to its every-
day use. Thus, in the case of loans with a maturity
of fifteen years, an interest rate of 3 percent or
less, and a grace period of five years, the element
of "grant" amounts to 43 percent when the cost of
money in the capital market of the lender countries
is 10 percent per annum, according to OECD and IBRD
estimates. Undoubtedly, the borrower benefits both
from the difference between the ruling and the sub-
sidized interest rates and from the grace period,
but the obligation of the recipient country to repay the entire loan remains and the foreign debt
burden is greater to the extent that it is not provided interest-free. The fact is that the volume
of free aid is appreciably less than one-third of
the total flow of financial resources to developing
countries. Moreover, loans granted in the recipient country's currency are included under the

heading of "grants," although this does not always
mean that this type of loan is not repayable. To
judge from the system operated in Greece, this concept does not correspond fully to reality. The
proceeds of these loans, accruing primarily from
the sale of U.S. surplus farm products, were transferred to counterpart funds in local currency and
used for payment of American expenses in Greece
(rents, salaries, American local administration
costs, and so forth). The only advantage of this
procedure for Greece was a saving in foreign exchange since to this extent the state budget was
repaying the loan in local currency. Why then consider these loans as "gifts"? In any case, it must
be emphasized that private flows of financial resources, accounting for half the aggregate development assistance, cannot even be regarded as normal
financing of the type practiced between economically advanced countries, since the credits are
granted on onerous terms. Still less can the title
"development aid" be applied to this class of private flows of financial resources.

Tied Aid

In contrast to the case with normal financing,
the loan resources made available to developing
countries generally speaking are not "free" since
the borrowing countries are unable to spend the
proceeds of these loans on purchases in world markets of their choice and to their best advantage.
The growing practice of aid-tying imposes the most
serious limitations on the flexibility of aid by
compelling developing nations to effect their purchases in the aid-giving country. Thus, aid-tying
imposes many different disadvantages on aid-
receiving countries since it compels them to purchase goods at prices often substantially above
those current in competitive world markets. Moreover, they have no control over quality while the
tying of shipping and insurance further adds to the
direct costs of such compulsory purchases within
the aid-giving countries. It has been estimated
that the system of aid-tying, which spread rapidly
in the 1960's, can reduce the volume of real aid
by as much as some 20 percent, while the great

administrative complications involved in the use of
tied aid cause serious delays in the real transfer
of funds and the preparation of plans. Tied aid accounts for about 30 percent of total official flows
of financial resources to developing countries.[7]

As a result of all these drawbacks, and of the
direct and indirect costs involved for the aid-
receiving countries, the effectiveness of development assistance is still further reduced. The system of aid-tying inhibits the expansion of trade
among developing nations and has serious effects on
their price structure and ultimately on their capacity to export to world markets. The accumulation of surpluses of foodstuffs, especially in the
United States, has contributed to the spread of
aid-tying. Other economically advanced countries
have followed the American example in this respect.
Moreover, the need to protect balance-of-payments
equilibrium has served as an argument for the extension of aid-tying, although aid-giving countries
also have tried to use it to exert political pressure on the aid-receiving nations.

It is most discouraging that the industrially
advanced countries still show no disposition to
abandon the regrettable practice of aid-tying. It
is true that at a meeting held in Tokyo in September, 1970 this group of countries declared, for the
first time, its willingness to adhere, in principle,
to an agreement for the "untying" of their bilateral
financial loans. However, no agreement was reached
as to the actual elimination of aid-tying. No date
has yet been fixed for the general untying of aid,
and no DAC member is willing to adopt this measure
unilaterally and without guarantees that others
will follow suit. It looks in fact as though real
action on this crucial question has been postponed
indefinitely.

THE OPPRESSIVE DEBT BURDEN

It is obvious that the present policy of development financing can only result in a rapid
growth of indebtedness, involving a heavy burden on

aid-receiving countries. Growth rates in the majority of developing nations in GNP per capita have
not exceeded an annual average of 2.5 percent over
the past decade.

At the end of 1969 the outstanding foreign
debt of developing countries totaled $90 billion,
made up as follows:

Public and publicly guaranteed debt	$60 billion*
Private debt	$30 billion**
Total	$90 billion

Total outstanding public external debt increased at an average annual rate of about 15 percent in the course of the 1960's and has thus doubled since the end of 1964. The growth of foreign
debt was twice as fast as the expansion in export
earnings since economic development requires an
ever-increasing volume of investment funds, especially during the crucial "take-off" stage. When
development financing is effected on unfavorable
terms, the adverse repercussions on the borrowing
country's economy soon become manifest.

Developing nations transfer large amounts of
funds to aid-giving countries each year in payment

---

*According to the World Bank (Annual Report
1970, p. 57), external public debt, which had almost doubled since the end of 1964, totaled $53.4
billion in 1968. On the basis of preliminary estimates of the World Bank, by the end of 1969 total
external public debt reached the $60 billion level
approximately.

**According to OECD, private investment and
lending totaled approximately $30 billion in 1966,
with as much as $14.5 billion representing direct
investment in oil production and other minerals.

of interest and amortization on their foreign debts.
The flow of debt service payments on official account amounted to $4.7 billion in 1968 and $5.2
billion in 1969.[8] This debt servicing weighs heavily on the debtor countries' state budgets, and
still more on their balance-of-payments position.
If the ratio of total public debt service and investment income payments to foreign exchange earnings from the export of goods and services is taken
as a criterion, the situation of several developing
countries is seen to be very serious. Thus, according to estimates prepared by the World Bank,
public debt servicing in 1968 absorbed the following proportions of such foreign exchange earnings:
Argentina, 27.8 percent; Mexico, 26.8 percent; Tu-
nisia, 24 percent; Peru, 20.9 percent; and Pakistan,
19.4 percent. But this is not all. To the public
debt service total of $5.2 billion in 1969 must be
added interest and amortization payments on private
flows of financial resources, namely investment and
loans. These payments are estimated to have amounted to approximately $6.3 billion in 1969 (see Ta-
ble 18).

In 1969, debt service payments on both official and private account by developing countries
amounted to about $11 billion and gross lending to
these countries to about $16 billion. Therefore,
the reverse flow of debt service payments as a percentage of gross lending averaged about 70 percent,
with the ratio varying from one major geographical
region to another. A United Nations survey indicates that the relation between payments for investment income and net inflows of long-term financial resources and official grants registered the
changes shown in Table 19. According to this survey, Latin America transfers to foreign creditors
5 percent more than it receives from them while the
seven oil-exporting countries pay out five times
more than they receive.

The problem of debt service has already
reached serious proportions and is expected to get
even worse in the course of the next few years.
Thus, by 1977 an average annual growth of 14 percent

TABLE 18

Gross Private Lending and Debt Service Payments
by Major Region, 1963, 1965, and 1967
(millions of U.S. dollars)

Region	1963	1965	1967
Latin America and other regions of Western Hemisphere			
Gross Lending	1,607.0	2,009.0	2,529.8
Amortization	1,234.3	1,444.8	1,786.3
Interest	372.7	564.2	743.5
Africa			
Gross Lending	267.4	682.6	861.4
Amortization	138.0	505.3	614.1
Interest	129.4	177.3	247.3
Middle East			
Gross Lending	1,269.4	1,357.0	1,646.8
Amortization	1,176.5	1,234.0	1,525.2
Interest	92.9	123.0	121.6
Asia			
Gross Lending	548.3	707.6	760.2
Amortization	244.3	268.1	299.0
Interest	304.0	439.5	461.2
All regions			
Gross Lending	3,692.1	4,756.2	5,798.2
Amortization	2,793.1	2,452.2	4,224.6
Interest	899.0	1,304.0	1,573.6

Source: UNCTAD document TD/B/C.3.73 of February 20, 1970.

TABLE 19

Average Annual Percentage of Debt Service
Payments to Gross Lending, 1965-67

Group of Countries	Percentage of Gross Lending
Developing countries (48, exclusive of oil-exporting countries)	49.3
Latin America (20 countries)	104.9
Africa (13 countries)	57.0
Asia (15 countries)	25.2
Oil-exporting countries (7 countries)	521.2

Source: UNCTAD document TD/B/C.3.73 of February 20, 1970.

in new lending, i.e., similar to that registered
during 1965-67, will raise the flow of external
debt service payments on official account alone to
$9.2 billion, compared with $5.3 billion in 1969.
Inclusive of debt service payments on private lending, which will probably be in the neighborhood of
$8 billion by 1977, it is clear that the outflow of
financial funds from the developing nations will
exceed the level of foreign aggregate gross lending
to them.

At this point we are faced with the paradoxical
situation that within a few years the poor nations
will be paying the rich countries more than they
receive from them in development assistance. This
can hardly be the objective that international development assistance was intended to achieve.

NOTES

1. An analysis of the repercussion of technological progress on developing countries can be
found in the report by Raul Prebish, then Secretary
General of UNCTAD, International Development Strategy (New York: United Nations, 1968). The need
for aid was equally considered by the Pearson Report, which underlines the moral obligation of the
rich to share with those who have not. However,
"concern with the needs of other and poorer nations
is the expression of a new and fundamental aspect
of the modern age--the awareness that we live in a
village world, that we belong to a world community."
See Partners in Development: Report of the Commission on International Development (New York:
Praeger Publishers, 1969), p. 8.

2. This point of view was elaborated in the
FAO Review CERES of January, 1970. The same issue
contains an article by Rene Dumont in reply to the
thesis of P. T. Bauer.

3. Total net flow of financial resources to
developing nations from the socialist countries of
Eastern Europe and Asia during the 1960's is shown
below (in millions of U.S. dollars):

1960:	200	1965:	325
1961:	300	1966:	350
1962:	400	1967:	350
1963:	375	1968:	325
1964:	375	1969:	350

Source: OECD, Resources for the Third World (Paris, 1970).

4. According to the Jackson Report, "as a
matter of historical interest, the idea of 'one
per cent' arose much earlier. It appears to have
originated with Mr. Harry Dexter White, after a
lunch with Lord Keynes in September, 1943, and was
applied to the UNRRA operations." See A Study of
the Capacity of the United Nations Development

System (Geneva: United Nations, 1969, Sales No.
E.70.I.10), Vol. II, p. 4.

5. According to the figures referred to in
Robert S. McNamara, President of IBRD, Address to
the Council of Governors, Copenhagen, September 21,
1970, p. 10.

6. According to OECD, the "grant element"
measures the extent to which the economic benefit
realized by the aid-receiving country exceeds the
real economic costs of the operation of the loan,
including interest charges and premium for risks of
default. The calculation of the grant element of a
given loan is effected by deducting from the nominal amount of the loan the discounted cost of future
flows of repayments of amortization and interest.
In the case of a straightforward grant, the "grant
element" is 100 percent. In the event of a very
low or zero interest rate and a very long maturity
period, the grant element is very substantial. By
contrast, whenever loans are contracted at high
interest rates and short maturity periods, the
grant element is negligible. A detailed analysis
of the concept of "grant element" can be found in
the following OECD publications: The Flow of Financial Resources to Less-Developed Countries
(Paris, 1967), p. 137ff.; Development Assistance
Efforts and Policies, 1968 Review (Paris, 1969),
pp. 293ff.

7. This percentage is mentioned in the Pearson Report. See Partners in Development, op. cit.,
p. 172. According to another study submitted to
the second UNCTAD, if prices in the lending countries exceeded the level of world prices by an
average of 15 percent, then the real interest rate
was higher than the world level by an average of
50 percent. See John Pincus, Growth and Development Financing, TD/7 Supplement (UNCTAD, October 10,
1970).

8. The changes in external public debt outstanding and debt service payments of 81 developing

countries from 1965 to 1968 are shown below (in
billions of U.S. dollars):

	Debt Outstanding Including Undisbursed, December 31	Service Payments
1965	37.8	3.4
1966	42.7	3.9
1967	47.9	4.2
1968	53.4	4.7

Source: World Bank, Annual Report 1970.

5

THE NEED
FOR A NEW
INTERNATIONAL
DEVELOPMENT
STRATEGY

THE RESPONSIBILITIES OF
DEVELOPING COUNTRIES

At this point it is advisable to mention some disturbing conclusions that emerge from the preceding chapters:

1. An immense gap exists between rich and poor countries.

2. This gap shows a persistent tendency to widen and is expected to do so significantly by the end of the century as compared with the 1970 level.

3. The average annual growth rate of 2.4 percent attained by the developing countries clearly is so inadequate as to keep the living standards of their populations at lamentably low levels.

4. The developed nations' unfavorable trade policies, combined with a steady rise in prices of manufactures, have caused an average annual loss of $2-3 billion in the foreign exchange earnings of developing nations, have accentuated their external imbalance, and are likely to push their balance of payments deficit up to $35 billion within the 1970's.

5. The developed nations are showing a growing indifference toward the development problems of
the Third World since, out of a global GNP (inclusive of that of the developed communist countries)
of $2,600 billion, they actually devote only $4.5
billion to development aid, or 0.18 percent of
their GNP. At the same time, these economically advanced countries are spending the vast amount of
$200 billion on armaments and $20 billion on space
travel each year.

6. The so-called development aid imposes an
oppressive indebtedness on the developing nations.
Already their debt servicing absorbs 70 percent of
new gross inflow, and in a few years' time it is
expected to exceed aggregate foreign aid and thus
reverse the direction of the present net flow of
financial resources.

In the light of these irrefutable facts, the
situation of the developing countries looks "deplorable," or "still pitifully low," to quote the
words used in the United Nations resolution of October 24, 1970, and calls for the formulation of a
new development strategy capable of stopping and
later reversing this alarming trend, which is leading developing countries to disaster.

Three Tasks of Overriding Priority

The realization of this major objective calls
for a new global development strategy that will ensure close coordination of national policies with
effective international action. In the elaboration
and application of this strategy, the developing
nations obviously must be expected to play a most
important role since economic development is primarily a national affair.

As regards the action to be taken, three tasks
head the list of priorities:

1. Preparation and application of bold and
realistic long-term development plans designed to

mobilize the dynamic factors of society, to provide
employment for the active population, to utilize
idle material and human resources, to profit by foreign technological progress, to assist in the promotion of active international cooperation, and, above
all, to assure an equitable distribution among the
whole population of the fruits of this collective
development effort.

2.   Adoption by developing nations of plans
for assuring the most effective and productive use
of foreign aid. Only on this condition can they
hope to accelerate the achievement of balanced
socioeconomic development.

3.   Close cooperation among developing nations,
and between them and the specialized agencies, thus
ensuring coordination of their respective efforts
and maximization of the advantages of such joint
action. Refusing to indulge in highly unrealistic
or even utopian designs, and adopting a rational
policy that excludes all wasteful use of scarce resources and all prestige projects, these nations
must launch a plan of concerted action based on
present-day realities and their priority requirements. In the field of developing financing, for
example, in all their negotiations with economically advanced countries and/or specialized agencies
priority should be assigned to securing an easing
of the existing foreign debt burden. It is truly
astonishing that developing nations have thus far
failed to formulate such a demand for easier foreign aid.

The rapid and effective realization of the essential preconditions for the social and economic
progress of the developing countries demands com-
plementary planning on both the national and the
international plane. National action will include
measures designed to mobilize domestic resources,
to develop agricultural production, to accelerate
industrialization, to exploit the new achievements
of science and technology, and to solve the problem of providing gainful employment for the whole

employable population. International action will
consist primarily in the adoption of foreign trade
policies that will promote the exporting possibilities of the developing countries, in measures aimed
at preserving balance-of-payments equilibrium (a
matter of critical importance for those countries),
and in arrangements to provide more effective financial and technical aid.

ACTIVE PLANNING FOR ACCELERATED DEVELOPMENT

The aim of the present study is not to examine
in depth all aspects of development policy. However, reference should be made here to numerous
studies undertaken by the various United Nations
departments and specialized agencies in preparation
for the Second Development Decade, as well as to
the resolutions adopted by the Economic and Social
Council, and, above all, to the General Assembly
Resolution of October 24, 1971, on international
development strategy for that decade. These studies, surveys, and resolutions will be of the utmost
importance in the preparation of economic plans for
the developing countries.

However, it is imperative to stress the dangers that would arise from any attempt to pursue
the socioeconomic development of low-income countries along classical lines. Action adopted should
be in conformity with the new conditions and exigencies that may be expected to mark the last quarter of this century.[1]

Here we would lay particular emphasis on the
following points to be taken into account in future
development policy: (1) appropriate type of planning, (2) rate of economic growth, (3) new bases of
international cooperation, and (4) methods of financing the countries of the Third World.

The Rationale for Planning

Let us look first at the problem of planning.
The preparation and implementation of an economic

plan formerly was regarded as a system peculiar to
centrally planned economies, and even as recently
as the 1950's opposition to planning was still very
strong in certain conservative economic circles.[2]

Today, however, the general attitude to planning is completely different, and even in the capitalist countries planning is widely regarded as essential for the acceleration of economic development. It is recognized that, without a thoroughly
prepared and effectively coordinated plan, reasonable growth rates cannot be achieved, nor can satisfactory social welfare conditions be established
by the state.

Planning is designed to maximize the use of
material and human resources so as to attain a number of objectives that are carefully classed in order of priority by the central authorities. It is
thus an indispensable instrument of economic policy
for achieving socioeconomic progress, and its adoption is accordingly an urgent necessity for all developing nations. Experience has shown that in the
absence of a development plan it is not possible to
achieve the desired degree of utilization of national resources or to carry out the essential institutional and administrative reforms without
which the entire effort to accelerate economic development may be a failure.

The type of planning to be adopted will depend
on the socioeconomic structure of the country concerned, its political system, and the stage of economic development already reached. The nature of
the planning will need to be modified as time
passes and development progresses. A plan suitable
for the initial phase of development will prove in-
appropriate at a later phase. Consequently, each
country must periodically appraise its own economic
situation, decide what new objectives must be pursued, and adopt the appropriate policy measures for
their attainment.

Development planning is therefore a function
of each country's social and economic structure.

The preparation and above all the implementation of
a plan often encounters formidable obstacles in
very backward countries where market mechanisms do
not operate smoothly, where statistical data are un-
reliable and public administration is defective, and
where large sections of the population live on the
threshold of poverty and starvation. On the other
hand, a more sophisticated plan will more effectively serve the requirements of a country that is economically and politically more advanced. This
point is of particular relevance since failure due
to planning that is ill adapted to the particular
conditions of a country will be a source of disillusionment for the population and will aggravate future difficulties.

It should not be forgotten that "the plan" has
a certain mythical quality that fires the imagination of the people. The population in poor countries is convinced that the plan has a miraculous
power of accelerating progress and eliminating poverty. They believe that it is economic planning
that has assured the rapid progress of European
countries and that, if the Soviet Union has succeeded within the space of 35 years in transforming
itself from a predominantly agricultural country
into the second industrial power in the world, this
has been made possible by the implementation of its
five-year plans. Therefore, the authorities must
attach due importance to this psychological factor
if they are to avoid the risk of serious repercussions on development.

Global or Sectoral Planning

Global planning covers all sectors of a country's economic activity and is the most advanced
form of development planning. It relies on econometric models for determining such key parameters
as aggregate saving, investment, private and public
consumption expenditure, employment levels, and
volume of imports and exports.

Sectoral planning, on the other hand, relates
to individual sectors of economic activity, and in

particular to the public sector, where state and
other public investment expenditure tends to be coordinated under a single overall plan. Numerous
experts assert that global planning is not desirable for developing countries because of the risk
of errors in calculation due to badly organized public administration and inefficiency in the collection of the data that are essential for the drawing
up of the various development projects.[3]

This assertion about global planning is true
up to a certain point, for the less developed nations do not possess an organization capable of
undertaking the planning, much less its execution.
However, the major limitation of sectoral planning
lies in the inability of the planners to appraise
a country's growth rate without possessing a comprehensive knowledge of its economic activities as
a whole. Moreover, on the restricted basis of sectoral planning it is difficult to estimate the comparative advantages of public and private projects
and thereby determine the role that each sector
should play in the overall development effort. For
these reasons, global planning is a superior instrument for long-term economic policy in that it permits
rational decision-making that would not be possible
on the basis of sectoral planning. Furthermore,
sectoral planning leads to numerous imbalances, especially between supply and demand, that may endanger the success of development policies.

The Advantages of Two-Sector Planning

Despite the obvious advantages, it is advisable not to overlook or underestimate the difficulties associated with global planning. A series of
surveys has cast doubt on the validity of the two
postulates on which the growth model is based,
namely the rate of investment and the capital/output
coefficient.[4] The United Nations Economic Commission for Africa (ECA) observed that one of the weaknesses of development planning is to attach undue
importance to investments in material resources as
the only policy tool for raising incomes.

In our opinion, the most suitable system of
planning for developing countries is one that would
combine the advantages of both methods while eliminating, as far as possible, their disadvantages.
Consequently, we consider that planning should be
divided into two sectors that must form an integrated whole: (1) an integrated and active plan of
public investment and (2) a flexible and indicative
plan of the private sector.

The active planning of public investment constitutes an essential prerequisite for accelerated
economic growth. Investment by the public sector
in infrastructure projects, in certain basic industries, and in public works in general tends to create a general climate of confidence and supplies
the prior conditions for the expansion of activity
in the private sector. In developing nations, the
steadily broadening scope of public investment, effected under the exclusive control of central authorities and public organizations, assures better
coordination of both the preparation and the implementation of projects within the context of the
plan. If the state is unable to coordinate and
supervise investment projects within its own field
of activity, how can one envisage a planning of
private activities that are outside the state's
control?

When too much attention is paid to perfecting
planning techniques, the preparation and execution
of public investment projects are often neglected
to the detriment of development policies. Nevertheless, planning public investment is no easy task
for the authorities since a great deal of work is
required to determine, on the basis of rational
criteria of priorities, the sectors in which investment is to take place; to find the necessary financial resources both external and domestic; and
thereafter to thoroughly supervise the execution of
the projects so that costly delays are minimized.
The central planning authority must devote its full
attention to the question of public investment,
given its central place in the overall development

effort.* Such countries as Israel and Mexico owe
their high growth rates to the efficient preparation of their public investment planning.

Planning the activities of the private sector
should be both flexible and indicative. Moreover,
it should be adjusted to private investment decisions, although within the context of social and
economic policy measures designed to guide private
activities toward desirable targets.

Improved public administration and better data
collection, together with the experience acquired
during the period of "trial and error," may reasonably be expected to permanently raise the quality
of development planning.

THE VITAL SIGNIFICANCE OF GROWTH RATES

Although one cannot regard national income as
the sole criterion of social and economic progress,
a rise in its growth rate is a precondition for improving living standards and other major constitu-
ents of development in its broadest sense.

The role of growth rates is in fact of crucial
importance. Thus, a yearly increase of 1 percent
in GNP will double it in 70 years, while a 4 percent increase will do so in 18 years and a 7 percent increase in only 10 years. The most striking
illustration of the significance of growth rates is
the phenomenal progress of Japan from 1963 to 1968,
during which period its GNP, industrial production,
and export trade doubled.

A slow rate of development does not permit the
utilization of idle material and human resources,

_____

*This viewpoint was particularly stressed by
the Commission under my chairmanship, which was entrusted with the preparation of the first five-year
plan of Greece before 1967.

the solution of the unemployment problem, and satisfactory improvement in the living standard. Moreover, it tends to increase the numbers of surplus
workers, to aggravate income inequalities, and to
intensify social unrest. Hence, for the most speedy
possible freeing of developing countries from poverty and misery, it is imperative to achieve high rates
of growth.

Certainly, a new country with unused material
resources and an ample supply of manpower is capable,
under certain conditions, of attaining high growth
rates. In any case, these will exceed the rates
currently achieved by rich countries which, having
arrived at economic and industrial maturity, cannot
always keep up the rate of growth that marked the
initial phase of their development. In his report
submitted in August, 1969, to the United Nations,
Jan Tinbergen, President of the Committee for Development Planning during the Second Development Decade,
proposed a 6 to 7 percent growth rate for all developing nations in order to assure an average annual
rise of 3.5 to 4.5 in per capita income during the
1970's. Mr. Tinbergen explained that one of the
reasons why the Committee decided to postulate rather ambitious rates of growth was that the gravity
of the employment problem--one of the major social
problems--was such that there could be no hope of
even partially solving it without adopting really
ambitious production targets.[5] This proposal of
the Planning Committee was endorsed by representa-
tives of the various international organizations
that participated in the work of the Preparatory
Committee of the United Nations for the Second Development Decade, convened in Geneva in August, 1969.

Inadequate as well as Difficult
Growth Rates

On the basis of these recommendations, the
General Assembly of the United Nations, in its resolution on the Second Development Decade, proposed a
minimum 6 percent average annual growth rate in GNP
as the objective for all developing nations during

that decade, with the possibility of fixing an even higher rate for the second half of the decade following a general review of the situation in the middle of the decade.[6]

According to this resolution, a 6 percent rate of growth in GNP would call for an average annual rate of growth of 4 percent for agricultural production and 8 percent for industrial output. Moreover, the realization of the 6 percent target would require average annual rates of increase as follows:

1. Average annual increases of 0.5 percent in the ratio of gross domestic saving to GDP, so that the ratio would reach about 20 percent by 1980,

2. Average annual increases of slightly less than 7 percent in the value of imports and slightly more than 7 percent in export earnings.

A minimum average rate of development of 6 percent annually in GNP would permit an average annual growth rate of 3.5 percent in per capita incomes in developing countries during the Second Development Decade, resulting in the doubling of present per capita incomes within a period of twenty years.

Although we regard the proposed rates of development as inadequate to assure a marked improvement in living standard in developing regions, we cannot but feel skeptical as to their feasibility in present conditions. Since developing nations attained an average annual per capita income growth of only 2.8 percent during the 1960's, is it possible that the rate of 3.5 percent per annum envisaged by the United Nations General Assembly could be achieved without a radical readjustment of the policies hitherto adopted? Admittedly, developing nations are now better equipped, especially as regards infrastructure projects, to embark upon an accelerated course of socioeconomic development during the Second Development Decade, and today they find themselves in a more favorable position to prepare and implement long-term development plans. As against this improved planning capacity, there is an increasing deterioration in economic and financial conditions as a result of the crushing burden of foreign indebtedness. This latter factor, if allowed to continue to have the same adverse influence as in the past, is bound to place serious obstacles in the way of accelerated development.

The Insufficiency of United
Nations Recommendations

Thus, the United Nations resolution concerning the Second Development Decade is limited to a formulation of desirable targets and theoretical recommendations without any suggestions as to concrete policy measures capable of extricating developing nations from their present impasse, especially in the field of foreign development assistance.

On the issue of financial resources earmarked for development, the United Nations General Assembly simply stresses that developing countries must continue to assume the major part of the responsibility for financing their own development. Furthermore, the resolution insists on the necessity of their adopting vigorous measures to mobilize their domestic financial resources.

As regards external development financing, the aforesaid resolution on "Development Strategy" repeats the injunction that each developed country should endeavor to transfer a minimum of 1 percent of GNP net at market prices each year and that a major part of these transfers, i.e., 0.70 percent of GNP, should be effected in the form of official flows (paragraph 42 of the resolution). However, there is hardly a single word in the resolution concerning real or free aid, the only type that could effectively assist the developing countries. This attitude implies that development assistance will continue to be provided on the same unfavorable terms as at present. Furthermore, the United Nations recommends that the developed nations endeavor to soften and harmonize the terms of aid in favor of

developing countries. This implies that, according
to another recommendation of 1965, re-endorsed by
DAC in 1969, 85 percent of official aid should include a minimum of 61 percent concessional element.[7]

No obvious concern is shown by the United Nations as to the necessity for an easing of existing
conditions which, as a result of the crushing burden
of debt service, will become intolerable in the near
future for the majority of developing nations. The
United Nations recommends that arrangements be per-
fected for anticipating and, if possible, preventing
balance-of-payment crises arising from foreign debt
service. Moreover, if such difficulties should
arise, the countries concerned should be willing to
solve them in a reasonable manner by resorting to a
whole series of possible methods including, if necessary, such measures as the rescheduling or refinan-
cing of existing debts on suitable terms (paragraph
47).

Thus, the United Nations remains vague in its
recommendations. It avoids any positive approach
to the problem of indebtedness and leaves the question of some possible future revision of debt arrangements to the care of the specialized agencies
and, above all, to the generosity of the aid-giving
countries.

The Advantages of High and
Realistic Growth Rates

There is no doubt whatever that radical measures are needed to deal with the existing situation, and that their implementation would facilitate attainment of the faster rates of development
that are indispensable if the living standards of
the developing nations are to be improved.

As emphasized above, only a considerable acceleration of growth rates will prevent further widening of the gap between the rich and the poor nations.
The enormous productive potential in human and material resources, together with the immense progress

in science and technology, makes it possible for
the new developing countries, at present far short
of the stage of economic maturity, to attain or even
exceed growth rates of 7-8 percent annually. These
targets would become easily achievable if appropriate measures could be adopted in the crucial field
of development financing. Such countries as Japan,
Israel, West Germany, and the centrally planned
economies have realized average growth rates of 7,
8, and even 10 per cent per annum during the past
two decades. Some typical average annual growth
rates of GDP in real terms for two periods are
shown in Table 20.

With the adoption of a new economic policy and
an assured flow of the necessary resources, it is
certain that developing countries could attain the
following growth rates: 7 percent in the 1970's,
8 percent in the 1980's, and 8.5 percent in the
1990's. The conditions necessary for the realization of these growth rates will be discussed in
Chapter 7.

TABLE 20

Average Annual Real Growth Rates of GDP,
Selected Countries, 1955-60 and 1960-70
(percentages)

Country	1955-60	1960-70
Japan	9.8	11.3
Israel	8.9	7.7
West Germany	6.3	4.7
U.S.S.R.	9.1	6.7
Yugoslavia	8.6	7.7

Sources: United Nations, Handbook of International Trade and Development Statistics (New York,
1969), pp. 172, 173; OECD, The Growth of Output
1960-80 (Paris, 1970), p. 90.

EXTENDING THE WELFARE STATE TO
THE INTERNATIONAL SCALE

Without effective international cooperation, the urgently needed radical socioeconomic policy measures to be adopted by developing countries will remain a dead letter. Economic development thus raises the question of international responsibility. This point of view was accepted by the United Nations General Assembly when it stressed that economic and social progress is a responsibility shared in common by the entire community of nations. However, the policy followed by the industrially advanced countries in the 1960's proved disappointing, and all the indications are that the situation will continue to deteriorate. Gunnar Myrdal, a world authority and for several years Secretary General of the Economic Commission for Europe, has stated: "In the Western developed countries there is an air of insincerity and even hypocrisy in the discussion of their relation with underdeveloped countries."[8]

Consequently, a new approach to the problem of socioeconomic development is essential if we seriously intend to break the present deadlock and stop the alarming widening of the gap between wealth and poverty that will lead to violent upheavals. If mankind is to survive and progress in a world of prosperity and peace, we must free ourselves of outdated ideas, understand the revolutionary spirit of the present day, and adopt a new policy animated by the spirit of international solidarity and based on the belief that prosperity is indivisible and that all peoples are members of one single community.

Such a policy is all the more urgent in view of the fact that the situation as regards the developing countries is steadily deteriorating and their deficits are progressively increasing. According to the most recent estimates made by the various specialized agencies as part of the preparations for the Second Development Decade, it can be reasonably expected that:

1.   The shortage of domestic savings relative
to the total investment requirements of the entire group of developing nations will be of the order of $27 to $34 billion in 1980.

2.   The foreign exchange deficit will be of
the order of $27 to $32 billion.

3.   If it were possible to cover part of the
foreign exchange deficit through the liberalization
of world trade and to replace imports by local products, foreign aid could then cover the major part
of the shortage of domestic savings.

Accepting the truth that world prosperity is
indivisible in the sense that rich countries cannot
survive indefinitely as islands isolated in an
ocean of misery, it follows that the problem of
prosperity is one that concerns mankind as a whole.
The new development strategy must entail a form of
international cooperation based on more realistic
principles if it is to promote the interests of the
entire community of nations. In relation to developing nations, the developed nations must adopt a
policy similar to that applied by them to their own
less privileged classes. In other words, the concept of the "Welfare State," namely, the redistribution of national income to raise the living standards of low-income sections of the population,
should be extended on a world scale. As Lord Bev-
eridge wrote in 1948, in his famous report on the
introduction of social security in Great Britain,
"the existence of want is an inexcusable scandal,
due solely to the fact one did not bother to take
the necessary measures to suppress it." Since
poverty, wherever it exists, "constitutes a danger
to the prosperity of all," as the Philadelphia
Declaration of 1944 proclaimed, why not do the utmost to extend to poor countries the postwar social
policy that largely abolished, or at any rate minimized, poverty and misery within the developed countries while at the same time accelerating the rate
of their economic growth? While social welfare
policies may not have produced all the results

expected from them, it is undeniable that they contributed to the improvement in living standards.
Could not their extension on a world scale help the
developing nations out of their present socioeconomic impasse? If we regard mankind as a community,
like a "village" (to quote the word used in the
Pearson Report), then the same social policy should
be applied to all countries of the world.

The transfer of an insignificant share of the
rich countries' resources, for example 0.50 percent
of their combined GNP, in the form of free aid to
developing nations over a certain number of years
would make possible the realization of a double objective:

1. To provide the volume of financial resources necessary to accelerate development rates,
thereby abolishing chronic poverty in the low-
income regions and setting them on the path of social progress;

2. To stimulate, through this redistribution
of world income, expansion of the productive capacity of developing regions and thereby raise the
buying power of their inhabitants. This, in turn,
would boost exports from economically advanced countries. Keynes' theory would thus find its application in a policy for the redistribution of resources
that would foster growth in all regions of the world.
It should not be forgotten that the Marshall Plan,
whose primary purpose was to assist the war-
shattered countries of Europe, also had a boosting
effect on the American economy which, at the cost
of an insignificant percentage of its GNP, initiated a process of continuous expansion.

Our proposal for assisting poor countries is
founded precisely on this principle. It is the
only rational policy that is both feasible and beneficial from a world point of view. Only by establishing effective international cooperation capable
of meeting the needs of the populations of the poor
regions of the world can we hope to create a

psychological climate suitable for mutual understanding and the peaceful and constructive coexistence of all peoples of the world.

This particular approach to the problem of economic backwardness is dictated by the principles of
international social justice. Who can deny that to
a large extent the wealth of the major industrial
countries stems from their economic domination over
developing countries whose raw materials feed their
huge industrial complexes? Can one be unaware that
certain products of underdeveloped regions are a
very important source of fiscal revenue for the rich
countries? A widely known case is that of oil and
its by-products, which provide substantial revenues
in all industrial countries since excise duties on
these products represent a large proportion of the
sales price. Could we not devote even an infinites-
imal share of these immense resources to assisting
poor nations? When shall we begin to realize that
we all belong to a single community of nations?

NOTES

1. The United Nations studies on the development strategy for the Second United Nations Development Decade, 1970-80, and in particular the Tinbergen, Myrdal, and Pearson reports converge on this
approach, despite certain reservation on some of
the specific points. The countries of the Third
World can greatly benefit by adapting them to their
requirements.

2. On the occasion of the publication of my
work Planisme et Progres Social (Paris: Editions
Durand-Auzias, 1963), in which I elaborated the
principle of the necessity for democratic planning
as a condition of socioeconomic progress, two of my
former professors, Gaston Jèze and Bruno Moll, expressed complete disagreement with my thesis. Gaston Jèze, the leading authority on the theory of
public finance, wrote the author: "Do I need to

tell you that I do not share your views! I am an orthodox liberal, attached more than ever to liberal principles. Your planning leads ultimately to slavery." For his part, Bruno Moll, in an extensive analysis of my work published in the Mexican Revue El Trimestro Economico (April-June, 1963), asserted that economic liberalism alone can assure progress, whereas planning leads to socialism and communism.

3. A. Waterson of the IBRD, after a long study of planning in general and planning in developing countries in particular, published an outstanding work on this subject. See French translation under the title La Planification du Développement (Paris: Edition Dunod, 1969). The author is highly skeptical about the effectiveness of global planning. Although he believes it is impossible to prove with certainty whether global planning is superior to sectoral planning during the initial stages of development, he concludes that "practical experience, however, together with commonsense, weighs decisively in favor of sectoral planning."

4. See Waterson, op. cit., pp. 75ff.

5. See United Nations, Preparatory Committee for the Second Development Decade, A/AC.141.L.8 of August 22, 1969.

6. Towards Accelerated Development (New York: United Nations, 1970), pp. 3ff.

7. See OECD, Development Assistance Efforts and Policies, 1969 Review (Paris, 1970). According to the Development Assistance Committee, "the concessional element is defined as the nominal value of the financing committed, reduced by the discounted concession of amortization and anticipated interest (using a discount rate of 10%)." On the basis of this definition, a loan with a maturity of 30 years and grace period of 8 years at 2.5 percent interest has a "grant" or concessional element of 61 percent.

8. See Gunnar Myrdal, The Challenge of World Poverty (New York: Pantheon Books, 1970), p. 311.

6

A NEW SYSTEM
OF DEVELOPMENT
FINANCING

RELIEF FROM EXISTING INDEBTEDNESS AS A
NECESSARY PRECONDITION

In the global development strategy broadly outlined in Chapter 5, financing is the precondition
for accelerated growth. Genuine development aid is
not only helpful but indispensable if backward countries are to be enabled to speed up their entry into
the category of developed countries. Without adequate outside aid, the pace of development will be
slow, and this may constitute a danger to world
peace.

Two Interrelated Procedures

Consideration of the most appropriate procedure
for instituting a new system of development financing must begin with a study of the various possible
ways of clearing up the present situation which, as
we have shown above, has been rendered untenable by
the accumulation of a crushing burden of external
debt.

However, it is not enough merely to take steps
to ease the present debt situation. It is equally
urgent to agree on satisfactory conditions for

future financing. These two necessities are so
closely interdependent that neither can be achieved
without the other. It is not sufficient to clear
up the present situation and then resume financing
on the previous unfavorable conditions. Sooner or
later, such half-measures would result in a recur-
rence of the same critical situation for the developing nations. Development financing on easier
terms will prove utterly useless if flows of external financial resources are absorbed in servicing
an oppressive legacy of debt from previous financing.
In a word, a simultaneous settlement must be found
for both these problems.

In a memorandum submitted in December, 1968,
to Robert S. McNamara, President of the IBRD, on occasion of the formation of the Pearson Commission,
I put forward certain proposals concerning the problem of development financing. The contents of this
memorandum, in a somewhat more extensive form, were
subsequently published in English under the title
Gold in the Service of the Developing Countries.[1]
I outline below the more important of these proposals, amplified where necessary in the light of
more recent developments.

Measures to Ease the Load of
Old Indebtedness

An easing of the outstanding debt burden is
the essential first step toward improving the present unhealthy situation. It is surprising that developing countries have not been more vocal on this
crucial point.

Measures to provide debt relief should be simple, uniform, and generous, and should apply to all
public or publicly guaranteed debts including those
in respect to loans from such specialized agencies
as the World Bank, the IMF, and the IDA.

As regards private debts, it would be advisable
to start negotiations between interested parties
with a view to arriving at a mutually acceptable

agreement. Such an agreement is indispensable in
order to safeguard the solvency reputation of each
debtor country and to maintain confidence on the
part of foreign lenders. However, a reduction in
the burden of private debt servicing is equally indispensable.

The overall terms of agreement should be formulated by a competent international agency. The
various debts of each country should be consolidated
in one or more new loans, on the following future
terms: interest rate of 2 percent, maturity in 40
years, with a grace period of 10 years.

Only on such terms as these could debtor countries benefit from an overhauling of the system of
development assistance and find it possible to
achieve faster development rates. Otherwise, in a
few years' time another round of negotiations would
become necessary, as has frequently happened in the
case of certain Latin American countries.

A proposal on the above lines logically should
meet with a favorable response since it is designed
to provide satisfaction for both sides. Thanks to
the alleviation of their debt burden, developing nations would benefit in much greater measure from
foreign aid and thus avoid an otherwise inevitable
financial crisis. The creditor countries should
find the proposed debt consolidation equally advantageous since, by thus assisting their debtors,
they would assure repayment in full of the funds
lent. If, on the other hand, the creditor countries refuse to grant their debtors genuinely essential payment facilities, they face the risk of suffering the consequences of ultimate default. Moreover, it should be recognized that the overindebted-
ness of developing countries is to a large extent
imputable to the rich countries which, in the case
of export credits, have often worked on prices more
than twice as high as those ruling in the world
market.

The proposed consolidation, which is designed
to reduce initial interest rates and prolong payment periods, is based on a system of financing often used between industrial countries. There is
the famous precedent of a $3,750 million loan by
the United States to the United Kingdom with a maturity of 50 years (1951-2000), an interest rate of
2 percent, and the provision that in certain circumstances payment of interest can be suspended or an-
nulled. Also, there are numerous instances of loan
agreements containing a special derogation clause
allowing debtor countries to defer payment of interest and principal for a certain period when faced
with balance-of-payment difficulties. The United
States also provided considerable financial resources, largely in the form of grants, to assist
several already developed West European countries
in the task of rehabilitating their war-devastated
economies. These are some instances of the application of the principles underlying the proposed revision of development aid policies. Why then, one
may ask, cannot what is regarded as legitimate for
certain industrial countries be equally extended to
developing nations that, under far worse socioeconomic conditions, are struggling to assure their
people freedom from want and hunger?

The Scandal of Development Aid

As stated earlier, on January 1, 1970, the outstanding external debt of, or guaranteed by, the
governments of all developing countries totaled
about $60 billion.[2] At first sight, this amount ap-
pears to be considerable. It is now instructive to
examine how this debt has accumulated over the years.
Since 1957 (the first year for which statistical
data were published by the various international organizations), official flows of financial resources
to developing countries have totaled $76.5 billion.[3]

Assuming that since 1957 the "gift" element in
total net official flows averaged about 60 percent,
or the equivalent of $46.5 billion,[4] the amount of
debt outstanding at the end of 1969 could not have

exceeded $30 billion. In the course of the same
period, developing countries made debt amortization
and interest payments to a total amount that may be
estimated at not less than $20 billion.[5]

The fact that, despite these "gifts" and the
large amount of debt service payments, developing
nations were still left with an outstanding external
indebtedness on the order of $60 billion at the end
of 1969 must appear inexplicable to the ordinary
mortal who is uninitiated in the mysteries of international development financing.

As we have seen above, this situation is due to
the fact that the "gift" element in foreign aid is
calculated in a manner that is not in accordance
with the strict sense of the word "gift." It is
used to cover not only genuine (i.e., nonrepayable)
grants but also financing on "soft terms." We have
seen that, according to the definition adopted by
the international organizations, a 15-year loan contracted at a "soft term" rate of 3 percent, with a
grace period of 5 years is regarded as containing a
43 percent "gift" element if the market cost of
money in the aid-giving country is 10 percent.
This "gift" consists of the difference between a 3
percent and a 10 percent interest rate, plus the
advantage of nonpayment of interest during the 5-
year grace period.

It is difficult to understand how international
agencies, whose mission it is to help developing
countries, have come to acquire this money-dealer
mentality, and are creating such misconception
about a problem of vital importance for the developing countries.

If there had been provision of genuinely "free"
development assistance that did not entail the payment of interest (a logical assumption when aid,
in the strict sense of the word, is given), the
outstanding external debt of all developing nations
should not have exceeded $10 billion by the end of
1969. How then can one account for the immense difference of $50 billion?

Obviously, the amount of $50 billion represents an astute camouflage of development financing, which has been presented to world public opinion under the deceptive guise of a "generous gift" when it is purely and simply a question of normal lending of the classical type, often on even more onerous terms, as when it is a case of "tied aid." The situation just described seems to justify the description of the scandal of "so-called development aid."

Possible Outcome of the Current Situation

Should developing nations be compelled to continue to bear such a crushing burden of foreign debt, the situation would soon become untenable and would inevitably culminate in a severe financial and economic crisis.

Ancient and contemporary economic history abounds in cases of heavily indebted countries that were forced, sooner or later, to announce their inability to meet their obligations--in other words, to declare themselves bankrupt. In the fifth century B.C., when the people of Athens were heavily indebted, the famous philosopher Solon was called upon to act as a mediator. To cope with the dangerous situation Solon introduced the "sisachty," namely, the cancellation by law of all outstanding debts. If creditors wish to escape so radical a measure as the "sisachty," their only course is to give timely consideration to the easing of the burden of old debt.

THE IMPACT OF ALLEVIATING THE
FOREIGN DEBT BURDEN

We will now seek to appraise the impact on developing countries of the alleviation of their outstanding foreign debt burden and the resultant saving in foreign exchange.

According to World Bank projections, servicing payments on the external public debt of 81 developing nations, totaling $5.2 billion in 1969, will rise to around $36 billion during the 1970's.[6] If we add the developing countries that are not included in this estimate, the aggregate debt service payments would be on the order of $40 billion at least. Thus, the initial consequence of the debt relief operation for Third World countries would be reduction of their budgetary burden and a saving of as much as $40 billion in foreign currency. Such substantial relief would enable the developing countries to accelerate the "take-off" of their economies under more favorable conditions.

The relief would be still more considerable if it were extended to also include private loans, where the situation is more unfavorable than that of the public loans. The private loans are estimated to have amounted to about $38 billion on January 1, 1970.[7]

Such a debt relief scheme would provide developing countries with financial resources to the amount of some $40 billion during the first decade, during which time those countries would be relieved of any payments for the servicing of their external public debt as a result of both the grace period of 10 years and the terms of the new financing system we propose. Up to the end of the grace period, these countries also would save about $2 billion annually since henceforth the interest rate on all consolidated old debts would be only 2 percent and the amortization periods would be longer.

CONDITIONS OF NEW FINANCING

After placing the settlement of outstanding foreign debts on a sounder basis, it is imperative to adopt a new system of development financing completely different from that in operation thus far.

Past experience has shown that the major obstacle to the acceleration of development, and the cause of the considerable financial difficulties experienced by the developing countries, is the crushing burden of interest and of short- and medium-term amortization payments.

The new plan of development financing that we propose should have the following major objectives:

1.   To provide developing countries, over a period of ten years, with loan funds totaling approximately $100 billion, of which about $40 billion during the second five years;

2.   To grant two-thirds of the total amount of these loans, interest-free, to the poorer developing countries, and one-third, at 2 percent interest, to medium-income countries;

3.   To fix maturities of 40 years and grace periods of 10 years for all loans;

4.   To abolish the system of "aid-tying" and replace it with a direct contribution by each industrialized country to an international agency;

5.   To entrust the administration and operation of the whole financing to an international institution, eventually the IBRD, after such reorganization as might be necessary to enable it to become the agency solely responsible for all development assistance operations. The creation of a single agency would be one of the essential conditions for the success of this plan;

6.   At the expiration of the 10-year grace period, to operate the new system of financing according to the terms and conditions that are customary among developed countries. As soon as the countries concerned have succeeded in overcoming all obstacles to their development and have started along the road toward self-sustained growth, they will no longer need development assistance on preferential terms.[8]

Some Clarifications

The abolition of aid-tying will make it possible to eliminate the political pressures inherent in bilateral agreements. Only then will borrowing countries have freedom of choice among world suppliers. In fact, this proposal has already been endorsed by the Pearson Commission, the DAC member countries, and the United Nations, although thus far industrialized countries have shown no disposition to fall in with this policy recommendation.

As to the objectives of the new development financing system--formulated initially in December, 1968, in a memorandum we submitted to the World Bank and the Pearson Commission--it is our firm belief that the flow of financial resources on preferential terms is the essential condition for productive cooperation between developed and developing countries with a view to accelerating the developing countries' social and economic progress. We have argued that the consolidation of outstanding external debts and the adoption of a new and more favorable development financing system must together provide the basis for development strategy on a world scale. Even the Pearson Commission admits that most of the developing nations have already reached the stage at which it is becoming impossible to assure foreign financing on commercial terms, and the Commission therefore recommends that "the terms of official development assistance loans should henceforth provide for interest of no more than 2 percent, a maturity of between 25 and 40 years, and a grace period of from 7 to 10 years."[9]

Although this recommendation did not meet with unanimous agreement and was not included in the general section of the Pearson Commission's report, it nevertheless reflects the recognition by the majority of the members of the Commission of the need to arrive at a system of financing on "soft" or concessional terms. Furthermore, in 1969 DAC adopted a recommendation inviting its member countries to ease their development assistance loan terms.

The widely accepted necessity of providing future development assistance on concessional terms must be formulated in a United Nations resolution, if possible of a mandatory character for all developed member countries.

The Role of the World Bank

A precondition for the success of the proposed financing policy is that the agency entrusted with the financing operations concentrate in itself all the powers and all the responsibilities associated with this task.

The lack of concerted action among the various bilateral and multilateral agencies largely accounts for the ineffective use that has been made of development aid, the greatly differing terms on which the aid is provided, and even for a great deal of wastefulness on the part of both the donor and the aid-receiving countries. The value and efficacy of the financing has been further reduced by complex and rigid administrative procedure.*

Under the system we propose, any developing country could enjoy the benefit of the concessional terms of financing by submitting to the aid-administering agency a plan showing the purposes for which aid was needed and guaranteeing that it would be effectively utilized for those purposes. It is only by means of such a rational system of financing, on the basis of a specific plan for the mobilization of all the material and human resources of each country, that the aid-receiving nations can accelerate their economic development.

---

*The list of regulatory conditions to be fulfilled in the United States in order to obtain a loan under the foreign aid program contains 68 different articles and continues to increase in number.

Countries refusing to accept this preliminary
procedure could always turn to other sources of financial assistance. Obviously, the operation of a
system of development assistance on "soft" or concessional terms involves the giving of certain prom-
ises by the borrowing countries with a view to ensuring the best possible use of the borrowed resources. However, such a system would not imply
any outside intervention in the domestic affairs
of the aid-receiving country.

The first question to be decided is whether
the World Bank is really the most appropriate organization for administering the new system of development financing or whether this task should be
entrusted to some other institution.

It would seem that the World Bank's approach
to the problems of development financing has given
rise to some apprehension. It is widely considered
to have operated in this context on ordinary commercial banking lines and not like a development-
financing agency.

The World Bank is criticized for not being suf-
ficiently concerned with the real objectives of development, for being too closely concerned with the
interests of the major industrial powers, and for
being excessively "Anglo-Saxon" in its management
and staff. Moreover, there has been criticism of
its slowness in examining investment projects and
coming to a decision as to their financing. Lastly,
there is a fear that the World Bank may be engaged
in too many and too varied activities for it to be
able to deal with all of them effectively.[10]

Of all the criticisms that can be leveled at
the World Bank, the most serious refers to the
severe terms imposed in its lending activities.
The Bank's loans are granted at an interest rate
of 7 percent and with a maturity period of 15 years.
Such terms mean a heavy burden of debt service and
thus leave nothing of the nature of aid proper in
this type of financing. According to official

records, only 38 percent of the funds advanced by
the World Bank (IBRD) and the International Development Association (IDA) are net transfers of financial resources to developing nations, the balance
being absorbed by debt service. This state of affairs is inconceivable in the case of international
agencies that are supposedly providing financial
assistance for developing nations.[11]

Nevertheless, since the World Bank has had considerable experience in the field of international
development assistance, since, despite the above
criticisms, it continues to enjoy a prestige superi-
or to that of other specialized agencies, and since
the proliferation of such agencies must be avoided,
the World Bank should in our opinion continue to be
entrusted with the administration of development
financing and be provided with the financial resources necessary to enable it to proceed with the
arrangement of such financing on concessional terms,
as we envisage.[12]

SOURCES OF DEVELOPMENT FINANCING

It remains now to consider ways of finding the
volume of financing resources required to operate
the proposed development assistance plan, i.e., to
provide the necessary capital flows and to cover
the financing costs, since in most cases the assistance will be granted in the form of interest-free
loans.

In the first place, an assessment must be made
of the volume of external development assistance
that will be required to enable developing countries
to cover their chronic balance-of-payments deficits,
which will be growing steadily in the near future.
The required volume of assistance will depend on
several factors, such as domestic savings levels,
the degree of development, and the absorptive capacity and effective utilization of foreign resources.
These factors vary from country to country.

In general, it may be said that the volume of
development assistance provided during the 1960's
was undoubtedly inadequate, totaling only $102 bil-
lion. The concessional or "grant" component in
this development assistance, although not in the
form of absolutely free aid, was 37 percent. Moreover, the aggregate amount of $102 billion must be
further reduced by 20 percent through direct and indirect costs, delays in transfers due to administrative procedures, and, above all, the manifold costs
imposed on borrowing countries by aid-tying prac-
tices. Consequently, developing countries received
and utilized foreign financial resources to a total
of not more than $4.5 billion annually, and this ac-
counts for their slow growth rates and for the serious difficulties with which they are confronted.

If the volume of development financing on concessional terms is to be adequate, it must average
some $10 billion a year over a decade. As explained
earlier, the rescheduling of outstanding debts would
relieve developing nations of $40 billion in debt
service payments if limited to public debts, and of
$60 billion if private debts are included.

These two policy measures, the new financing
and the economy of the rescheduling of outstanding
debts, would assure developing countries of financial resources on the order of $140 to $165 billion
over a whole decade, that is, an average annual
amount of some $15 billion, an amount that, if used
in accordance with carefully prepared and well implemented ten-year plans, should enable these countries to accelerate growth rates and achieve real
progress in all sectors of the economy.

Since, out of the total amount of financing,
$40 billion represents a reduction in the cost of
servicing old debts, it remains to devise methods
of raising the balance of about $100 billion for
development financing over the entire decade, or an
average annual sum of $10 billion. This sum would
take care of the positive aspect of the proposed
new system of financing.

In our opinion, the problem does not, in itself, present any serious difficulties. Here we
are identifying two potential sources of development
financing, one principal and the other supplementary.

According to repeated UNCTAD recommendations,
each industrialized country should extend to developing countries financial aid amounting to 1 percent of its GNP. The implementation of these recommendations would have supplied financial assistance
totaling some $17 billion. However, if we assume
an average annual growth in GNP of 5 percent, the
funds required for the proposed financing plan
could be provided by earmarking only 0.5 percent of
GNP, or half the UNCTAD target, on condition that
this financial contribution is given gratis.

This would be in conformity with the basic
principle of the new policy that we are proposing,
namely, the application by developed countries to
poor countries of the system of redistribution of
national income that the developed countries operate internally for the improvement of the living
standards of low-income sections of their populations.

The adoption of such a foreign aid policy by
the rich countries should not encounter any opposition whatsoever, since financial aid already provided amounts to 0.37 percent of their GNP, and a
few years ago financial flows in the form of "grants"
reached 0.5 percent. The failure of this financial
aid to achieve the expected results was largely due
to the defects inherent in the aid-tying system.
Other contributory factors were the irrational allocation of aid, the absence of a single aid-
administering international agency, and, above all,
the extremely hard terms of other assistance granted
to developing nations. Moreover, experience has
shown that, apart from political pressures, grants
provided directly by donor to beneficiary countries
in general have encouraged the recipients to waste,
misuse, or misapply these external resources. On
the whole, such bilateral grants tend to foster an

attitude of iresponsibility in their utilization,
whereas assistance loans provided by an international agency and under specific conditions compel
borrowing countries to make the best use of these
resources since such loans are ultimately repayable.

For developing countries, the essential is not
merely to obtain a larger volume of external assistance but equally to ensure more effective administration and utilization of the development assistance they receive. These countries will willingly
undertake to repay long-term foreign loan capital,
provided they are freed from high interest charges
that lead to the accumulation of a crushing indebtedness and ultimately to incapacity to honor com-
mitments.

Our proposal is specifically designed to eliminate all such difficulties and to make the financing more efficacious for the borrowing countries.
Instead of a scheme of direct flows of financial
resources from developed to developing countries,
we set out below a plan for the channeling of external resources to developing countries through
the intermediary of the World Bank, with suggestions
as to the procedure.

THE OPERATION OF THE NEW FINANCING SYSTEM

The proposed new system of financing would be
operated according to the following basic principles:

1. The World Bank must be extensively reorganized so that it can assume the role of a central
bank for development financing. In other words, it
will be the sole international institution author-
ized to grant loans on "soft" or concessional terms
and to coordinate the financing activities of other
specialized agencies, activities that will take place
under the Bank's direct supervision and control.

2. The government of each developed country
should include in its annual budget an amount

equivalent to 0.50 percent of the GNP for the preceding year and transfer this amount to the credit
of an account kept in the books of the World Bank
under the title "Fund for the Financing of Developing Countries." The amounts thus transferred will
thereafter be applied by the World Bank to the
granting of interest-free loans to low-income developing countries and loans at concessional interest rates to medium-income developing countries.

3. Each developing country desiring to take
advantage of the new system of financing must apply
to the World Bank for a loan and submit to it a
plan showing the proposed utilization of the loan.
This plan must form part of a long-term national
development plan approved by the competent central
authorities. After examination of the application,
the World Bank will decide whether it can or cannot
authorize the applicant country to purchase the
goods and services it requires from the country or
countries of its choice.

4. Each enterprise in a developed country
that is directly or indirectly approached by the
authorities of a developing country for the pro-
curement of goods and services will be paid by its
own government. Thereafter, that government will
apply to the World Bank for reimbursement of the
value of goods and services supplied by a transfer
of the relative amount from the "Fund for the Financing of Developing Countries."

5. Under the proposed financing plan, not
only will poor developing nations be able to obtain
interest-free loans but, at the end of the grace
period, additional operational funds will be created
with the World Bank, designed to assure development
financing on a permanent basis. This new development fund will be formed through the recovery, at
the fixed maturity dates, of capital loaned and
such interest as may be payable.

By this method, it should be possible, at the
end of ten years, to terminate this type of free

development aid, which today is absolutely essential. Furthermore, industrialized countries could modify their contribution commitment, based on a percentage of GNP, if recourse to an alternative source of free development financing became possible.

The new system of development financing may be expected to have favorable repercussions on the economies not only of the aid-receiving countries but of the donor countries as well. The improved import capacity of developing nations is bound to stimulate production and exports by industrial countries, which frequently subsidize their exports in order to maintain the expansion of their economy. In other words, the proposed financing plan will act in the same was as a new Marshall Plan, except that those to benefit will not be developed but developing countries, while the aid-giving countries will include all market economies, instead of the United States alone as under the original Marshall Plan, and eventually even the centrally planned economies. The fact that each developed country's contribution will be made in the form of goods and services, and not in freely convertible foreign exchange, in no way implies indirect aid-tying since each borrowing country will be entitled both to buy the commodities it needs and to choose the supplier.

One should not underestimate the interest that each developed country would have in stimulating its economy through the proposed system of financing, which assures so many benefits to developing nations. The ideal solution of course would be to establish a development fund in dollars, or any other convertible currency, and not in capital goods of each contributing country, especially in view of the possibility that a certain number of credits granted may remain unutilized. Such a disadvantage in the proposed system of financing could be remedied by means of triangular or multilateral arrangements.

NOTES

1. Angelos Angelopoulos, Gold in the Service of the Developing Countries (Geneva: Nagel Publishers, 1969).

2. According to World Bank figures, the outstanding public debt of 78 developing countries has registered the following changes over three selected years 1961, 1965, and 1968 (by main region and total, in millions of U.S. dollars):

	Total	Africa	Asia
Dec., 1961	21,587	3,309	5,336
Dec., 1965	37,065	6,618	11,743
June, 1968	47,542	7,952	16,074

	Latin America	Middle East	Southern Europe
Dec., 1961	8,822	1,419	2,261
Dec., 1965	12,207	2,446	4,051
June, 1968	14,754	3,543	5,118

3. OECD, Development Assistance Efforts and Policies, 1969 Review, p. 343.

4. According to DAC, from 1961 to 1969 official flows of financial resources totaled $63.1 billion, of which $37.6 billion, or about 60 percent of the total flows, is considered as "grants" and grant-like contributions. See OECD, Development Assistance Efforts and Policies, 1970 Review.

5. According to World Bank estimates, external public debt service payments of developing countries in 1967, 1968, and 1969 totaled $14.1 billion (see World Bank, Annual Report, 1970, p. 57). By adding $6 billion annually for the entire preceding period when the external public debt service payments were smaller, we arrive at an approximate global figure of $20 billion.

6. See World Bank, op. cit., Table 10, Statistical Annex, p. 52.

7. According to the OECD and IBRD estimates, total private investment and lending outstanding at the end of 1969 totaled about $37 to $38 billion. See World Bank, op. cit., p. 54.

8. The first proposal for financing of economic development under favorable terms was made by David Horowitz, presently Governor of the Bank of Israel. The proposal was submitted to the first UNCTAD conference held in Geneva in 1964 and thereafter was studied and commented upon by a World Bank committee of experts. Although our proposed system of financing differs on many points from that of Mr. Horowitz, it should be acknowledged that the Horowitz Plan induced the competent services of the international agencies to take into serious consideration the need for development financing on favorable terms. See The Horowitz Proposal: A Plan for Financing Economic Development of the Developing Countries, Selected Documents (Washington, D.C.: IBRD, November, 1965).

9. See Partners in Development: Report of the Commission on International Development (New York: Praeger Publishers, 1969), pp. 164ff.

10. Similar criticism has been expressed by the Pearson Report, namely that the World Bank should continue to assume responsibility for the study of development projects and thereafter entrust their implementation to other agencies. See Partners in Development, op. cit., p. 219.

11. The following are the figures of development financing for the years 1965-68 (millions of U.S. dollars):

Total flows, gross	4,070
Amortization	1,380
Total flows, net	2,690
Interest received	1,165
Transfers, net	1,525

See World Bank, op. cit., p. 53.

   12.   In his reply to the criticism by the
Pearson Commission, Robert S. McNamara, President
of IBRD, stressed in his address to the Board of
Governors in Copenhagen on September 21, 1970,
that "the true remedy would be to adjust the policy
of the Bank."

7

**A SUPPLEMENTARY
SOURCE
OF FINANCING:
THE REVALUATION
OF GOLD**

SHOULD GOLD BE REVALUED?

Another potential source of considerable financial aid that could be made available to developing countries is an eventual revaluation of gold.

For the reasons set out in a memorandum we submitted to Robert S. McNamara in December, 1968, we believe that sooner or later the revaluation of gold will become inevitable.[1] The course of events since that memorandum was written tends to reinforce this view. Moreover, monetary experts have persistently predicted serious complications in the functioning of the international monetary system, such as those we are now witnessing.

What we would stress here is that the fundamental cause of the succession of world monetary crises lies in the fact that international monetary problems--as is exactly the case with the problems of social and economic development--are not dealt with under a global long-term plan based on the ideals of international cooperation, mutual understanding, and human solidarity, but by recourse to short-term makeshift expedients.

Whether we like it or not, gold will long continue to play a predominant role in world monetary policies. Nowadays, when the impact of psychological factors on the world economic and monetary situation is stronger than ever, when inflation has become a chronic disease, and when the ratio of gold to total reserves is constantly falling, banks are striving to maintain large gold stocks. If gold is to fulfill its proper function, its price should be adjusted from time to time--say at intervals of 20 to 30 years--and aligned both with the price level of other commodities and with the rate of world economic development.

Economic history has repeatedly shown that, if an obviously necessary adjustment in the price of gold is too long delayed, confidence in the world monetary system begins to wane, speculation becomes rife, world currencies become unstable, and crisis follows crisis. These were the phenomena that marked the beginning of the 1930's. The attachment of governments to the dogma of the immutability of the official price of gold was still absolute at that time, although lack of confidence in the stability of leading world currencies was becoming increasingly manifest. On August 5, 1931, John Maynard Keynes wrote to Ramsay MacDonald, then British Prime Minister, these prophetic words: "It is now nearly certain that we shall go off the existing parity at no distant date. When doubts as to the prosperity of a currency, such as now exist about sterling, have come into existence, the game is up."

The devaluation of sterling was not long delayed, and soon afterward, in January, 1934, Franklin D. Roosevelt, President of the United States, decided to raise the official price of gold by about 70 percent. This revaluation had particularly favorable effects on economic progress and international liquidity. Moreover, it created a comforting revival of confidence in the leading world currencies, especially in the dollar, which was maintained until 1960. Around 1960-61, however,

that is to say at the close of a period that had
lasted almost 30 years, confidence in the stability
of the price of gold began to waver. Toward the
end of 1960, the price of gold rose to over $40 per
ounce on the London bullion market and the Bank of
England was forced, in agreement with the American
monetary authorities, to sell considerable quantities of gold. This action, together with Russian
sales of gold, restored the price to its former
level of $35 per ounce. If at that time the cen-
tral banks of the eight leading industrial countries had decided to revalue gold instead of setting up the Gold Pool in November, 1961, they would
have avoided the subsequent series of monetary
crises which resulted in considerable quantities of
gold passing into the hands of speculators and
hoarders whose purchases were officially reported
to have amounted to $3 billion during the period
November, 1967, to March, 1968. Had a timely decision to revalue gold been taken, the general economic and monetary situation would not have developed into the state in which it finds itself today.
Confidence in the dollar and other currencies would
have been restored, international liquidity considerably reinforced, and the prospects for social and
economic progress during the coming decade greatly
improved.

Just as Keynes persistently stressed the necessity for action during the 1930's, today we are
hearing serious warnings about the precarious state
of the international monetary system, with perhaps
even greater emphasis on the urgency of taking en-
ergetic measures to safeguard world monetary stability. A report published in December, 1968, by a
committee of UNCTAD experts warns that "the present
international monetary system remains highly vulnerable to sudden attacks on confidence" and that
therefore measures should be taken "to cope with
this situation which is most unsatisfactory for
monetary stability and economic progress."[2]

Nevertheless, despite all the danger signals
and the alarmingly deteriorating trend of the

economic and monetary situation, the old "classical" mentality (laisser faire, laisser aller) still survives, creating an atmosphere of indecision in which the responsible policy-makers continue to seek to improvize short-term solutions for long-term problems.

The various policy measures adopted, and in particular the system of Special Drawing Rights (SDR), not only are powerless under present conditions to solve the problem of international liquidity or to ensure monetary stability but will make the entire monetary system still more vulnerable. The monetary crisis in the summer of 1971 was further evidence of the precariousness of the situation.

EQUITABLE DISTRIBUTION OF THE GAINS FROM REVALUATION OF GOLD

The capital question we must now examine is not whether gold should or should not be revalued but who, if gold were revalued, would be entitled to the resultant plus-value.

In our opinion, a number of arguments of a social, economic, and moral character support the view that this plus-value should not accrue in its entirety either to the central banks of gold-owning countries or to those countries themselves.

In the first place, by virtue of an international agreement, the official price of gold has been maintained at $35 per ounce for the past 37 years, the last revaluation having taken place as far back as 1934. The Bretton Woods agreements of 1944 contemplated a world monetary system that would be based not only on gold, the dollar, and the pound but on the gold exchange standard. Thus, dollars side by side with gold, were recognized as "reserve currencies." All other currencies have established their parities in relation to both gold and the dollar.

If the price of gold had been allowed to align itself with the price level of other commodities, it would by now have risen to about double the official price, for world prices of other commodities have more than doubled since 1934.[3] By virtue of international agreements based not only on economic considerations but also on political expediency, the price of gold has been artifically maintained at a fixed level. Consequently, central banks have acquired gold at a price below that which would have prevailed if market conditions for gold had been similar to those for other metals. If later on it is decided, by international agreement, to normalize the price of gold, the resulting plus-value should in no case accrue entirely to the central banks that hold the gold reserves: the gain should belong to the world community as a whole.

The Role of the United Nations

On grounds of social justice, the plus-value created by the revaluation of gold should be distributed equitably. A revaluation that had the effect of enriching the industrial countries alone would violently shock public opinion, particularly in the developing countries. Can one possibly envisage a doubling of the price of gold with the resulting plus-value on the order of $54 billion accruing exclusively to the central banks? Surely a revaluation on such terms would be unthinkable. In fact, the equitable distribution of the plus-value is an indispensable precondition for any revaluation of gold. In our opinion, an equitable arrangement would be one under which a minimum of one-third of the gain was to be used to assist the financing of developing countries. In other words, when the revaluation takes place each central bank should transfer one-third of the plus-value that accrues on its gold reserves to the "Development Fund" at the World Bank.

Such a transfer of one-third of the plus-value accruing from the revaluation of gold really

amounts to a tax on this gain, imposed, by virtue
of the principle of international solidarity, in
order to provide assistance for the world's poorest
nations. Such taxation is fully justified. In all
countries, gains resulting from "automatic" appre-
ciation in the value of certain assets (such as a
rise in land values due to a growing demand for
housing or the execution of public investment projects) or cessions of private enterprises (in favorable conditions) are heavily taxed by the state
since these gains derive from socioeconomic development and cannot be related to a specific private
effort on the part of the owner or owners of such
assets. By the same principle, should not tax be
levied on the gains arising from a revaluation of
gold? The answer is definitely in the affirmative.
In this case, however, it is the state that will
stand to benefit from a profit not attributable to
domestic or national action but to an international
act affecting the whole world. If it is decided to
make the long overdue revaluation of gold, which is
the international authority or organization best
fitted to take over and administer part of the gain?

The United Nations is, in our opinion, the
agency best suited to perform this supranational
role in the domain of taxation. We therefore believe that all developing countries should ask the
United Nations General Assembly to adopt a resolution proposing that, in the event of a gold revaluation, one-third of the resultant plus-value should
be automatically transferred to the World Bank to
be used in providing financial assistance for the
developing countries.

The Role of the United States

Another possible solution, more realistic and
more practical, would depend primarily on the
United States, if it wishes to fulfill its role as
a great industrial power without allowing itself to
be influenced by narrow and short-term considerations. The role of the United States in the solution of the world's great economic problems is

paramount and will long remain so for the simple
reason that it produces 53 percent of the global
income of the non-communist developed countries and
that nothing on the required scale could be achieved
without American collaboration. However, there is
a feeling that the United States remains on the de-
fensive and is disinclined to put forward a constructive, equitable, and effective plan for getting out
of the present impasse and fostering a continuous
process of expansion on a world scale.

We believe that the United States should take
the initiative for a revaluation of gold coupled
with an equitable sharing of the resultant plus-
value in favor of the poorer countries. Our attitude is based on the following reasoning: Any revaluation of gold, which in any case will sooner or
later become inevitable, would be quite profitable
for the countries of Europe and for Japan but much
less so for the United States. When in 1934 President Roosevelt revalued the price of gold by 70
percent, a step whose repercussions were very favorable for the world economy as a whole, the
United States held 42 percent of the world's gold
reserves. Today it holds only 24 percent. Consequently, an unconditional revaluation of 25 percent
--which would correspond roughly to an alignment
with the present free-market price of gold--would
give the United States a plus-value of only $2.3
billion, whereas the gain to the other countries of
the West would be on the order of $10.5 billion. A
70 percent revaluation would leave the United
States with a gain of only $6.5 billion, whereas
other Western countries would benefit to the extent
of $23 billion.

If, on the other hand, the United States took
the initiative and put up the gold price by 70 percent and decided to devote a third of the plus-
value to the financing of the poor countries, this
American initiative, whose consequences would be
borne for the most part by the other industrialized
countries, would enhance the prestige of the United
States in the eyes of the countries of the Third

World, where at present it is somewhat in need of
reaffirmation. Furthermore, by such action the
United States would, as it has so often in the
past, demonstrate its readiness to take the lead in
bringing about a solution, in the general interest,
of great world problems.

For the utilization of this part of the plus-
value, the procedures would be the same as those
followed in the case of the contribution by each
individual government. As explained earlier, a
gold-owning country's obligation to transfer one-
third of the plus-value to the World Bank will not
have to be met either in gold or in freely convertible currencies but in the form of goods and services.

This form of transfer to developing nations of
one-third of the gains from the revaluation of gold
will have an anti-inflationary effect, whereas a
straight and uncontrolled revaluation would create
serious inflationary pressures. Moreover, even for
central banks it might be made mandatory to place
the balance of the gain from the revaluation of
gold at the disposal of the IMF to be used under
its control to bring about a progressive improvement in international liquidity.

THE ADVANTAGES OF A 70 PERCENT REVALUATION OF GOLD

In the event that a revaluation of gold came
to be regarded as indispensable for the promotion
of monetary stability and social and economic progress throughout the world, at what new level should
the price of gold be fixed?

The supporters of the revaluation of gold can
be divided into two groups: the first group favors
a 100 percent increase in the official price,
bringing it up to $70 per ounce, while the second
proposes a more modest increase of, for example,
30 percent, which would raise the official price to
$45 per ounce.

Neither of these proposals is entirely satisfactory. A very steep revaluation would enable speculators to make immense profits, contrary to the principle that the gains from this operation should be equitably distributed. On the other hand, too limited an increase in the price of gold would have a negligible effect on the world monetary system which, after a brief interval, would revert to its present vulnerable position.

Our proposal is a compromise between these two approaches. It contemplates a 70 percent increase, namely the same rate of revaluation as was adopted by President Roosevelt in January, 1934. Faced with the enormous economic problems created by the 1929 crisis, President Roosevelt raised the official price of gold from $20.67 to $35 per ounce. A similar rate of revaluation would raise today's official price of gold to $60 per ounce. Moreover, the Roosevelt precedent might well induce President Nixon and the U.S. Congress to take a similar step. It should be recalled that the 1934 revaluation had very favorable effects on both the American and the world economy, and made it possible to maintain international monetary stability over a period of about 30 years.

The following are the main advantages that would result from an upward adjustment in the official price of gold such as we advocate:

1. A satisfactory solution of the problem of international liquidity. The creation of new monetary reserves through the proposed gold revaluation would stimulate international economic activity and would facilitate the adjustments necessary with a view to the elimination of balance-of-payments deficits and/or surpluses.

2. An increase in world gold production, which has long remained virtually stationary. A rise in gold output would make it possible to increase official gold reserves which, for a certain time, would continue to be indispensable since nowadays confidence in the world monetary system presupposes

confidence in both gold and the reserve currencies.
This general confidence is the essential precondition for a rational long-term solution of the problems arising from the world's present monetary system.

3. Complete elimination of the nefarious activities of gold speculators. Speculation, encouraged by the artificial price of gold, tends to un-
dermine confidence in the stability of currencies
and to create a climate of uncertainty conducive to
price fluctuations and monetary crises, which inhibit world economic progress.

4. Utilization of part of the plus-value resulting from revaluation to finance the developing
countries, which will have a twofold stimulating
effect on world economic activity. On the one hand,
developing countries will be able to acquire, on
very favorable terms, the external resources they
need to help them overcome the monetary and balance-
of-payment difficulties that have brought them to
the verge of bankruptcy. On the other hand, their
import capacity, reinforced by adequate foreign financing, will have a powerful boosting effect on
the economic activity of industrial countries. It
is hardly necessary to add that the proposed system
of financing poor countries would be a free aid operation by the rich countries, involving no real
loss for them: on the contrary, it would stimulate
their industrial production and exports since the
aid-receiving countries' share in the plus-value
would be made available in the form of capital
goods required for the accelerated execution of
their economic development plans.

5. The progressive demonetization of gold,
which should be the ultimate aim of a rational monetary policy.

Let us therefore hope that gold ("that relic
of barbaric times," to quote Keynes), before being
demoted to the rank of an ordinary commodity, will
render one last service to mankind by transforming
itself into an instrument of rapid economic growth,

for poor and rich nations alike since prosperity is
truly indivisible.

PROBABLE PLUS-VALUE ARISING FROM THE REVALUATION OF GOLD

In order to determine what plus-value would
result from an upward adjustment in the price of
gold, it is necessary to arrive at a broad estimate
of the world's gold reserves. The calculation is
fairly easy so far as the gold reserves of the
Western world are concerned, but as regards the
communist countries it cannot be more than a very
rough approximation.

According to the figures of the Bank of International Settlements for the end of 1970, official
gold reserves held by central banks and international agencies in non-communist countries totaled approximately $41 billion, distributed as shown in
Table 21.

In the event of a 70 percent revaluation all
gold reserves (inclusive of those of Eastern bloc
countries, estimated at approximately $13.2 billion)
the resulting plus-value would amount to about
$37.8 billion and the one-third share of developing
countries to $12.6 billion. If the contribution is
limited to the gold reserves of central banks of
the Western world, the financial resources available for the proposed financing plan would be cut
to $9.5 billion.

Special Tax on Gold Production

The gains from the proposed gold revaluation
would not be confined to the gold reserves held by
central banks but would also include gold-producing
countries as well as speculators and hoarders, who
could realize enormous "windfall" profits.

In order to neutralize at least a part of
these gains, it would be necessary to reduce them
by a special tax. If, for instance, a 70 percent

TABLE 21

Distribution of Gold Reserves of
Non-Communist Countries, 1970
(millions of U.S. dollars)

Country	Gold Reserves
United States	11,070
United Kingdom	1,350
Other non-communist countries in Western Europe	
West Germany	3,980
Belgium	1,470
Denmark	65
France	3,530
Ireland	15
Italy	2,890
Netherlands	1,790
Portugal	900
Sweden	200
Switzerland	2,730
Other countries	1,175
Total	19,245
Elsewhere	
Canada	790
Japan	535
Latin America	1,085
Middle East	970
Rest of the world	2,135
Total	5,515
Total for all countries	37,180
International agencies	4,100
Grand total	41,280

Source: Bank of International Settlements,
Forty-first Annual Report (Basel, 1970), p. 156.

increase in the price of gold were decided upon and
the new official price were fixed at $60 per ounce,
then the following annual tax should be imposed:
25 percent for the first three years and 15 percent
for the subsequent four years. Thereafter, the
special tax should be abolished.

Under the proposed scheme, the special tax on
the gains from a gold revaluation would also be designed to assure the progressive restoration of
normal monetary conditions. Therefore, its application should be of limited duration and its rate
gradually reduced.

In our opinion, the levying of a tax on gold
production does not present any serious difficulties since it is a question of tax at source. However, there would have to be an agreement among
world monetary authorities and gold-producing countries prior to the revaluation. The agreement
would stipulate that all gold-producting countries
will deliver their gold output to the IMF or to
central banks and will accept payment for it at the
official price less the tax, namely at $45 or $51
per ounce according to the period of sales. The
balance of $15 or $9 represents the amount of the
special tax and would be transferred automatically
to the "Development Fund" account with the World
Bank.

Recent experience supports the view that world
monetary authorities are capable of arriving at
such an agreement. Moreover, the gold-producing
countries do not seem opposed to such taxation.
Indeed, they would have every interest in accepting
it since it would allow them a sufficient margin of
profit and, moreover, give them an incentive to ac-
tivate gold mines that have long remained idle because, at the present official price of gold, re-
ceipts no longer covered working costs.

South Africa, which accounts for about 75 percent of the total gold production of the non-
communist world, has already expressed agreement in

principle with this proposal in a letter sent to me
by the Minister of Finance, N. Diederichs, after
the publication of my book <u>Gold in the Service of
the Developing Countries</u>.[4] Commenting on my proposals regarding the revaluation of gold, Mr.
Diederichs expressed certain reservations as to the
practicality of the special tax that I envisaged
but added that "these reservations are of relatively minor importance." If the Soviet Union, the
other main gold-producing country, could also be
induced to accept the proposed principle of a tax
on output, the entire operation of gold revaluation
would be facilitated and the plan of financing the
progress of developing nations on favorable terms
would become a reality.

The Position of the Soviet Union

It might perhaps be argued that, should the
communist countries remain aloof and refuse to take
part in the proposed scheme for taxing revaluation
gains, the implementation of the entire project
would be rendered difficult since the Soviet Union
ranks second to South Africa among the world's
leading gold-producing countries.

If the Soviet Union rejected the principle of
the taxing of the plus-value on gold, this act
would have adverse effects both on its prestige in
the eyes of the developing nations and on its own
real economic interests since, if it refused to
participate in assisting the developing countries
by supplying, as counterpart of one-third of the
gain accruing to it from the revaluation of gold,
goods and services essential to their development,
it would leave the way open for the Western industrial countries to profit by this situation to the
detriment of the interests of communist countries.
Logically speaking, therefore, the Soviet Union
should not be opposed to the adoption of such a financing plan, not only as regards the contribution
of its share of the plus-value on gold but equally
as regards the contribution of 0.5 percent of its
GNP.

At a time of intensifying competition for export markets, will the countries of the Eastern
bloc allow themselves to be left out in the cold?
Can they passively accept the loss of their trade
outlets in the Third World and the severance of
their economic and other ties with it?

In the present climate of international détente,
it does not seem impossible that the Eastern bloc
countries may seek broader cooperation with the
Western world in the sphere of monetary policy.
There is already talk of the possibility of participation by the Eastern bloc countries in the IMF.
If this possibility became a reality, it would
greatly facilitate the implementation of the proposed financing plan.

Sales of Gold on the Free Market

In my book <u>Gold in the Service of the Developing Countries</u>, I envisaged the levying of a tax on
sales of private holdings of gold on the free market
(by speculators, hoarders, and so forth).[5] We had
thought that the creation of a new "Gold Pool"
would have assured a control over these sales and
the collection of the tax. However, after further
careful consideration we have come to the conclusion that it is advisable to abandon this idea for
the following two reasons:

1. The collection of this tax would be difficult and would create confusion and complication
detrimental to the smooth working of the international monetary system.

2. Most hoarders of gold have held it for a
number of years, particularly in the case of France
and other European countries. Their hoarding has
resulted in a loss of income that other forms of
investment would not have entailed. Persons who
have held gold for ten or more years--and this is
quite frequently the case--might have earned at
least 60 percent on their initial capital if they
had invested it more judiciously.

Projected Yield for Development Financing

A 70 percent revaluation of gold could provide supplementary financial resources for the
"Development Fund" as follows:

1. One-third of the plus-value accruing on
the gold reserves of all central banks: $12.7 bil-
lion. (If limited to Western countries only, the
contribution from this source would be $9.6 bil-
lion.)

2. An estimated $3.1 billion yield over a pe-
riod of seven years from the tax on new production
of gold calculated on the average annual output of
1967-69. If the Soviet production of gold, estimated at $600 million per annum at the present of-
ficial price, were included, the total yield of the
tax on the plus-value would be $3.8 billion.

3. Thus, the total supplementary financial
resources for the "Development Fund" provided by a
70 percent revaluation of gold would be $16.5 bil-
lion. This yield would be reduced to $12.7 billion
if the communist countries did not participate in
the scheme.

THE ROLE OF SPECIAL DRAWING RIGHTS
IN FINANCING DEVELOPMENT

Although the revaluation of gold is undoubtedly one way out of the present monetary crisis, it
would not appear that the United States, the major
determiner of world monetary policy, is at present
contemplating such a solution. The U.S. administration takes the view that the "dollar standard"
can replace the gold exchange standard and that for
the time being gold can be relegated to second
place. According to the Americans, the problem of
international liquidity is moving toward an interim
settlement on the basis of the Special Drawing
Rights (SDR) scheme, already in operation. Although we are not among the partisans of SDR, we

believe that SDR might, for a certain time, serve
as an international reserve currency because the
free market price of gold is substantially above
the official rate. Since the free market for gold
came into operation, the price has gone up from $35
to around $43 per ounce. Isn't the SDR scheme in
fact a disguised revaluation of gold?

Assuming that the real price of gold should be
$43-44 per ounce, or 25 percent above the official
price, then the latent, but real, plus-value on the
central banks' gold reserves would amount to $10
billion. Since the contemplated amount of SDR to
be allotted during the first three years is $9.5
billion, it might be argued that this amount corresponds almost exactly to this latent plus-value.
Consequently, we believe that the SDR will be accepted with almost the same confidence as the other
reserve currencies, since in fact it represents a
value covered by this latent plus-value.

There is a risk that in the end the SDR scheme
might turn out to amount to a disguised revaluation
of gold, the unavowed aim having been the indirect
alienation, in favor of the rich countries, of the
whole of the revaluation gain, in which, for reasons discussed above, the developing countries are
equally entitled to share. The operation of this
scheme could, within a few years, result in the accumulation of SDR to a total of $35-40 billion, or
double the value, at the official price of gold, of
the gold reserves held by central banks. At that
juncture, the monetary authorities might at last
decide to revalue gold in order to finally reabsorb,
to the benefit of the industrial countries, what
nowadays is called "paper gold."

Faced with the prospect of such an eventuality
--which would really be the result of a sort of
"rich countries' conspiracy"--what should be the
attitude of the developing countries? The Third
World nations should simply demand that one-third
of the SDR be handed over to the "Development Fund"
at the World Bank. Specialized agencies, such as

UNCTAD, IDA, and others, should take the initiative
in "selling" this idea. In this context, one must
welcome the recommendation, in a report prepared by
a group of 14 United Nations experts representing
diverse trends of opinion, of the linking of the
creation of SDR with the provision of development
aid as both feasible and desirable.[6] Although not
recommending as radical a measure as we propose
(namely, the mandatory allocation of one-third of
the volume of the SDR as a free gift to increase
the resources of the "Development Fund" at the
World Bank), the group of experts envisages a more
flexible policy that, under certain conditions,
could contribute to the provisional solution of the
problem of financial assistance to developing countries. However, we doubt whether the group's recommendations will have any positive results because
they are vague as regards the volume and nature of
development aid. Their report does not make clear
whether it is referring to free aid or assistance
loans. Moreover, it leaves decision on these matters to the discretion of the developed donor countries, to the exclusion of the developing countries.

In any case, the creation of the SDR cannot be
expected to provide an effective solution of either
the problem of international liquidities, a matter
that principally concerns the developing nations,
or the pressing problems posed by the world monetary system.[7] It should not be forgotten that only
a revaluation of gold on a plan such as we have
outlined above could have the desired favorable effects on economic growth, on international liquidities and the monetary system, and, last but not
least, on the flow of financial aid to developing
countries.

NOTES

1. See Angelos Angelopoulos, <u>Gold in the Ser-vice of the Developing Countries</u> (Geneva: Nagel Publishers, 1969).

2. Among the numerous economists who in the last few years admitted the necessity of a gold re-valuation, one should mention Jacques Rueff, who has been persistently warning those responsible for monetary policy of the impasse toward which they are heading by neglecting to adopt an effective monetary reform. See his latest work, <u>Le péché monétaire de l'Occident</u> (Paris: Plon, 1971). Of the most recent works dealing with the problems of gold and those of the world monetary system, we should mention Milton Gilbert, <u>Problems of the International Monetary System</u> (Princeton, N.J.: Princeton University Press, 1966); Randal Hinshaw, ed., <u>Monetary Reform and the Price of Gold</u> (Baltimore: Johns Hopkins Press, 1969); J. L'Huillier, <u>Le Système Monétaire International</u> (Paris: A. Colin, 1971); Charles Kindleberger, <u>Power and Money</u> (London: Macmillan, 1970); F. Machlup, <u>Remaking the International Monetary System</u> (Baltimore: Johns Hopkins Press, 1968); Robert Mossé, <u>Problèmes Monétaires Internationaux</u> (Paris: Payot, 1969); Tibor Scitovsky, <u>Money and the Balance of Payments</u> (London: Allen and Unwin, 1969); Robert Triffin, <u>The Evolution of the International Monetary System</u> (Princeton, N.J.: Princeton University Press, 1964); Xenophon Zolotas, <u>The Gold Trap and the Dollar</u> (Athens: Papazisis, 1968) and <u>Speculocracy and the International Monetary System</u> (Athens: Papazisis, 1969).

3. In an article published in the review <u>Monde Uni</u>, October, 1969, André Piatier approves of my proposal to revalue gold and transfer part of the gains to developing countries, and asserts that this money can and should assist the Third World nations. Moreover, when discussing my proposals, F. Baudhuin (see <u>La Libre Belgique</u>, December 13, 1969) arrived at the conclusion that the Angelopoulos Plan, which

has original ideas on the subject of gold, is certainly better than the present inaction which poses dangers of collapse for the world economy. Anthony Babel, for his part, writes that "this audacious plan could have the most desirable social and human consequences," while Fred Bates states (*Tribune de Genève*, December 15, 1968) that "this work opens new possibilities and new perspectives in the study of this important problem."

4. Angelopoulos, *Gold in the Service of Developing Countries*, *op. cit.*

5. *Ibid*.

6. See *International Monetary Reform and Cooperation for Development: Report of the Expert Group on International Monetary Issues* (New York: United Nations, 1970), p. 27.

7. See Angelos Angelopoulos, "La signification des DTS," *Le Monde*, March 8, 1970.

8

PRECIPITATING FACTORS
IN THE EMERGENCE
OF THE THIRD WORLD

THE ROLE OF SCIENTIFIC AND
TECHNOLOGICAL ADVANCES

The view has been widely expressed in the industrial countries that it might perhaps be advisable to reduce development aid so as to slow down the economic growth rate of developing nations and thereby keep within bounds the role they play on the international stage. Supporters of such a view cite various instances of wasteful use of foreign aid and underline the shortcomings and mistakes of developing countries in the implementation of their economic policies. In this way, doubt is created as to the very principle of economic aid to the Third World. This change in attitude has become clearly manifest in the United States since the return to power of the Republican Party which, within the space of two years, cut down foreign aid programs by 50 percent. The pessimistic forecast of The New York Times has thus proved to be accurate. An editorial of January 5, 1969, entitled "Requiem for Foreign Aid," contained these prophetic words: "The United States foreign aid program, once a robust model of enlightened self-interest, has been reduced to a skeleton in recent years by a series of 'bare bones' presidential budgets and congressional

surgical operations. Now it appears that the Re-
publicans are preparing to bury the bones."[1]

By now it should be abundantly clear that any
policy that opposed assistance to the developing
countries would be misguided and even dangerous.
It would be misguided because social and economic
development is the major objective of the Third
World countries, whose determination to attain it
is unshakable and will, sooner or later, be rewarded
with success even if the rich nations cut down their
aid or even cut it out altogether. It would be dangerous because, in addition to being incapable of
preventing the economic growth of the Third World
countries, such a policy would jeopardize the capital already invested in those regions by the rich
countries and because, in the resulting climate of
suspicion and vengefulness, sooner or later there
might well be open and violent conflict between
rich and poor countries.

The economic development of the Third World is
an irreversible process, and the countries that are
poor today will succeed in catching up on their
great backwardness within a shorter space of time
than it took Western countries to reach their present stage of prosperity. Three factors justify
this assertion: (1) the immense advances in science and technology, (2) the enormous manpower potential of today's poor countries, and (3) the generalization of education and the dynamic role of
youth. Let us briefly consider the importance of
these factors.

Technology, which is the systematic application of science and of advancing experience in the
field of organization and management of national
resources, both material and human, has always
served man as an effective instrument for accelerating economic development. Although man's economic condition changed only very slightly over
three thousand years, the invention of the steam
engine revolutionized everything. Thus, between
the date of that invention and the year 1900, labor

productivity increased twofold. In the succeeding
half-century, it doubled again thanks to the use of
electricity and oil. Again, from 1950 to 1970, i.e.,
within the space of only 20 years, productivity in
certain countries once more doubled, and in others
even trebled. This phenomenal progress has been
brought about by the scientific and technological
revolution of our times, and is exerting an ever-
growing influence on the economic growth of all
countries.

Development Through Science

Science is a powerful instrument of progress
nowadays. The advance in knowledge resulting from
the widening of educational facilities is playing a
crucial role in economic growth. E. Denison has
calculated that 42 percent of the growth in real
national income per employed person in the United
States from 1909 to 1967 is attributable to improvements in education, and 36 percent to the advance
in technical knowledge.[2] This is why developed
countries devote enormous sums to scientific research and to the practical application of its results. Research and development (R & D) are inter-
related concepts, and the advancement of knowledge
is generally regarded as an essential precondition
for economic growth.[3]

For the time being, the contribution of scientific and technological progress is of much greater
significance in the advanced than in the developing
countries. In countries that are still at the
stage of extensive development, a process involving
a considerably intensified use of the labor factor,
the scope for the application of technological advances is limited. On the other hand, in countries
that already have reached the stage of intensive development, technological advances play a predominant
role. According to a study prepared by the Economic
Commission for Europe, the contribution of technical
progress to the growth in the GNP of eight countries
of Western Europe from 1949 to 1959 ranged from 51
to 75 percent.[4] On the other hand, in the developing

countries, and especially those in Asia and Africa where the degree of economic development is very much lower, the role of technological progress can only be extremely limited, at least for the time being. Nevertheless, in time, modern scientific and technological advances are bound to be increasingly helpful to developing countries. With an adequate infrastructure and an ample supply of manpower that is gradually acquiring the necessary skills, these countries, although "late in the field," are actively preparing to enable themselves to derive the maximum advantages from the technological achievements of developed countries.

Impact of World Divisions on Scientific Progress

Two factors tend to accelerate the economic development of emergent nations: (1) technical innovations are now adopted and applied much more rapidly than previously, and (2) the "latecomers," the nations that are only now setting out on the road toward industrialization, can acquire the most up-to-date equipment, which will enable them to compete in world markets.

In earlier times, especially after the appearance of monopolies, scientific and technological advances found their industrial or other practical application only with a certain time-lag so that the losses resulting from obsolescence of existing machinery or equipment should be minimized. To give a few examples, the number of years that elapsed between the following inventions or discoveries and their practical application was: for the telephone, 55 (1820 to 1875); for radio broadcasting, 35 (1867 to 1902); for radar, 15 (1925 to 1940); and for television, 12 (1922 to 1934).

After World War I, and even more after World War II, when the division of the world into two ideological blocs became greatly accentuated, technological innovations began to be applied at a much faster pace than ever before. If the world had not

been thus divided, atomic power and computers would
not have become an integral part of industrial life
so rapidly.[5]

The fear about too rapid an industrial adoption of new types of energy by a country that still
possessed adequate conventional sources to a large
extent explains the initial slowness in the industrial application of atomic energy in the United
States. In an article published in Le Monde in
September, 1952, I wrote that the United States
"cannot delay the industrial use of atomic energy
if another country, for instance the Soviet Union,
succeeds in using it." In a second article later
published in the same newspaper, I emphasized that
mankind "awaits--after the awesome race from the
atom bomb to the hydrogen bomb--the announcement of
what we may be able to call 'the productive bomb,'
that is, the harnessing of this colossal force to
serve the promotion of world prosperity."[6]

This "productive bomb" did not take long to
"explode." On June 27, 1952, the Soviet Union an-
nounced that the first atomic power station, with a
5,000 kilowatt capacity, had been put into operation. In the same year, the United States launched
a vast scheme to generate electric power from nuclear fission, and that country still leads the
world in this field.

Humanity is still hopefully awaiting the announcement that thermonuclear energy has been har-
nessed for industrial and other peaceful uses. As
we wrote in the book, Will the Atom Unite the World?,
this new source of energy is destined to transform
the geopolitical map of the world.[7] When man succeeds in "domesticating" thermonuclear energy,
which up to the present has been used only in the
manufacture of the hydrogen bomb, the task of the
developing nations will be immensely facilitated by
the availability of an inexhaustible source of energy. If he can confine his activity to peaceful
objectives, man will even be able to melt glaciers
and irrigate deserts.

The Chinese Experience

What is certain is that nothing can prevent
the immediate application of scientific and technical advances. The entry of the People's Republic
of China into the "atom and space travel club" is
bound to accentuate competition in this field. The
case of China is highly significant and instructive.
This vast country, with huge resources still unexploited, has managed to make a scientific "leap forward" and is fast overtaking the other nuclear powers. This achievement proves that, by mobilizing
its material and human resources and coordinating
its efforts, a developing country can, in certain
fields, catch up with the industrially advanced
countries in a much shorter time than has hitherto
been believed possible. Whereas it took the United
States 13 years to advance from the explosion of
its first atom bomb to the launching of its first
satellite, and 8 years for the Soviet Union, China
has achieved this scientific and technological advance in less than 6 years.

It would thus be a great mistake to believe
that any one country can indefinitely hold a scientific monopoly, for science knows no frontiers,
fatherland, race, or ideology. As early as 1945,
Gordon Dean, the first Chairman of the U.S. Atomic
Energy Commission, made this significant remark:
"The secret that people have discovered, other
people can discover in their turn. To that effect
what is required is nothing else but intelligence,
'know-how,' ability and material resources, namely
all the elements over which no nations, no group of
nations, can preserve a monopoly."[8]

Future Scientific Advances

Developing nations are not relying exclusively
on the utilization of technological advances already
achieved but more on those anticipated for the last
quarter of this century. American scientists and
technical experts in various fields claim that,
within the next fifteen years, the human race will

succeed in solving some of its most challenging
problems thanks to an unprecedented rate of technological progress. They have even drawn up a "timetable for progress" by sector and by year, covering
the industrial use of atomic energy, the utilization of the vast resources of the oceans, the production of new types of electronic equipment and
computers, the fight against the pollution of atmosphere and water, and the mastery over cancer and
other diseases. According to this timetable, by
1975 the problem of seawater desalination will have
been solved--an achievement of capital importance
for the irrigation of deserts and arid lands. These
same research workers predict that the industrial
application of thermonuclear energy will probably
be realized during the decade 1985-95, while advances in the electronics field within the next fifteen years will eclipse the entire progress of the
last twenty years.[9]

THE IMPACT OF POPULATION

On the assumption that a country's national income is determined by the level of employment, the
long-term outlook for developing nations is very
promising provided productive employment can be
found for the active labor force.

Modern machinery and equipment incorporate the
latest technological advances and enormous increases
in productivity seem assured. The Third World nations are thus pursuing their social and economic
development under the most promising conditions
since, out of a world population of 3.6 billion in
1970, the active labor force accounted for 1.5 billion, of whom 1 billion lived in the developing
countries. By 1980, the active labor force in these
countries is estimated to reach some 1.25 billion.[10]

The world's active labor force, that is to say,
persons in the 15-64 year age group, totaled about
2 billion in 1970 and is expected to reach around

2.5 billion by 1980 and 2.9 billion by the year
2000.[11]

Projections of world population for the years
1970, 1980, and 2000, grouped under the headings of
developed and developing countries irrespective of
social system, are shown in Table 22. According to
the projections in Table 22, the active labor force
of the Third World is expected to grow from 1.6 billion in 1970 to nearly 3 billion by 2000. In other
words, at the end of the century, 83 out of every
100 persons of working age will be living in developing countries, and only 17 in developed countries.
Moreover, according to the same projections, in
2025, by which year population will have doubled
again, the developed countries' share of the world's
active labor force will be even smaller. It is
therefore easy to visualize the impact of such an
enormous potential labor force, not only on economic
development but in particular on the world balance
of power.

TABLE 22

World Population Projections for Selected Years
(millions)

Region	1970	1980	2000
World			
Total population	3,584	4,344	6,112
Active labor force	2,093	2,536	3,545
Developed countries			
Total population	1,114	1,200	1,441
Active labor force	457	503	605
Developing countries			
Total population	2,470	3,144	4,671
Active labor force	1,636	2,033	2,940

Source: World Economic Survey, 1968, Part I
(New York: United Nations, 1969), pp. 8, 9.

Admittedly, the contribution that can be expected from this huge mass of workers will depend on how capable governments are of making the best use of these human resources. This entails, first, creating adequate opportunities for gainful employment and, second, raising the productivity of labor by vocational training and the generalization of education.

Meanwhile, chronic unemployment and underemployment are at present characteristic features of developing countries. Although it is difficult to ascertain with any precision the number of unemployed in these countries, one can, as does the ILO, put the figure at 7.5 percent of the active population as a rough estimate. Although this estimate is probably on the low side, it indicates that in 1970 the total number of unemployed was around 76 million.[12] Taking as a basis the population of working age, the same percentage would bring the number of unemployed up to some 122 million. These figures do not take into account the chronic underemployment that afflicts almost all developing countries.[13]

The problem will be aggravated by the anticipated increase of about 226 million in the active labor force between 1970 and 1980. This increase will mean that employment opportunities should be found for an active labor force totaling some 300 million, or for about 500 million persons if calculated on the total population of working age.* The most pressing problem is how to provide work for this additional active labor force while endeavoring to cope with the existing unemployment and underemployment situation. Admittedly, the solution of this crucial problem presents serious

*In the developing countries, the population of working age is expected to grow during the 1970's at an average rate of 2.7 percent as opposed to 1 percent in the industrially advanced countries.

difficulties, first because technological and structural changes increase production faster than they
create jobs, and second because the average annual
growth rate of the GNP of developing countries is
inadequate. An average annual growth rate of at
least 7-8 percent would be required for the progressive solution of the unemployment problem.

Can the developing nations succeed in this
task? The ILO is optimistic and has just launched
a "World Employment Program" designed primarily
to help developing countries cure unemployment and
achieve full employment, a task both difficult and
urgent.[14] Without underestimating the numerous difficulties to be overcome, the ILO believes that the
efforts undertaken by certain international agencies will enable developing nations to achieve their
objective as regards the improvement of the employment situation much more quickly than did the already developed countries.

The time it will take to achieve these objectives will largely depend on the will and ability
of the ruling classes in the developing countries
to adopt effective employment-promoting policies
within the framework of a vigorous and realistic
long-term plan, and to a lesser extent on the understanding shown by the industrial countries whose
role it is to provide the necessary international
cooperation and assistance. One thing, however, is
certain: the peoples of the developing countries
are not going to remain passive in the face of failure by their leaders to extricate them from their
present demoralizing state of enforced idleness.

THE ROLE OF THE YOUNG GENERATION

In the process of far-reaching transformation
of existing institutions and social, economic, and
administrative structures, the young generation in
the developing countries will play a decisive role.*

----

*According to the definition adopted by the
United Nations, the term "youth" applies to all
persons between the ages of 12 and 25 years.

The young will become "the agents and the benefi-
ciaries--not the victims--of development," and for
the realization of the ideals and aims of the United
Nations it is imperative that youth show interest
and participate actively in national life and international cooperation.[15] These general directives of
the United Nations testify to the necessity of asso-
ciating the youth of the Third World with the search
for solutions to problems that are of direct concern
to them, and are bound to exert a growing influence
on them. In the developing nations, the young generation is becoming increasingly conscious of its
numerical strength, its responsibilities, and the
role it must play not only within its own country
but also on the international scene.

The following facts must be taken into account
if we are to understand the situation with regard
to the young generation in all countries, and particularly in the developing countries:

1. Over half the world population--54 percent--
consists of persons under 25 years of age.

2. A world total of 770 million persons in
the 12-25 year age group forms what is called "the
young generation." This total is distributed very
unequally: more than three-quarters of the total,
or about 600 million, live in the developing countries, and more than half this number in Asia.

3. It is estimated that the number of young
people in the 12-25 year age group will reach the
billion mark by 1980. Of this world total, developing nations will account for about 700 million,
and 875 million by the year 2000.

Thus, the role of the young generation in the
development efforts of the Third World countries
will be of growing importance since, in addition to
their sheer weight in numbers, these young people
are increasingly keen on improving their general
level of education and vocational training; are
taking an increasingly active part in social, economic, and political life; and are vigorously (often violently) voicing their demands, especially in

regard to reforms in education, in public health
services and, above all, in employment promotion
policies.

However, the young generation is not satisfied
with the mere formulation of new policies; it
presses for their immediate and effective implementation. The fact that youth today is often angry
and disputatious is due to a sense of frustration
at seeing its demands and aspirations ignored by
the decision-makers. The widening of the "gap" between the young and the adult generation results
from a deep cleavage of opinion as to the role that
the one and the other should play in our complex
modern society. Youth feels itself thwarted by social institutions established and run by older
people within a rigid social system in which youth
has no say on policies that will profoundly affect
its own future.

Progress in Education

It must be recognized that in most cases the
governments of developing countries, acutely conscious of their responsibilities, are endeavoring
to extend the facilities for general education and
vocational training, and to plan work projects that
will create increasing employment opportunities for
young people and thus fit them to play their part
in the national effort to achieve social and economic betterment.

Although many problems still must be solved before the overall employment situation can improve,
substantial advances have been made in the field of
education. In most of the developing countries,
educational and vocational training facilities have
been considerably extended and improved, although
here too much remains to be done. Between 1950 and
1965, the number of children entering primary school
rose at an average annual rate of 7.7 percent in
Africa, 6.3 percent in Asia, and 5.6 percent in
Latin America. Furthermore, various developing
countries are striving to reduce the percentage of

illiteracy by providing elementary education facilities for adults.

Although some progress has been made, educational levels in developing countries still leave
much to be desired. The proportion of children not
attending school is in the region of 40 percent,
while the number of drop-outs during the first
years of primary education averages about 50 percent of total enrollment. It has been estimated
that in 1962 the number of young people above school
age, i.e., in the 15-24 year age group, totaled 146
million while the illiteracy rate in certain developing countries was over 50 percent.[16] On the whole,
the number of illiterates has continued to increase,
and in 1970 had reached over 800 million, as compared with 700 million in 1950.

Despite the difficulties referred to above,
the extension and reorientation of the educational
systems of the developing countries will have to
continue for some decades if there is to be any possibility of creating the large body of scientific
and technical personnel who will be indispensable
for the assimilation by those countries of the immense advances currently taking place elsewhere in
science and technology, and for the optimum utilization of the material and human resources of each
country.

The Third World's development prospects thus
appear very favorable. The important thing is that
these countries are beginning to realize what education means for their development, and that year
by year they are devoting an increased amount of
funds to the expansion and improvement of the educational system. Thus, it is estimated that the
combined expenditure of developing countries on
education rose at an average annual rate of 12.5
percent from 1950 to 1965, as against a rise of
only 6.5 percent in the developed countries.[17] The
proportion of total public expenditure devoted to
education each year in the developing countries
varies from 14 to 17 percent, or about the same

proportion as is found in developed countries. The
future evolution of the educational system will
largely depend on the determination and ability of
the relative authorities to cope effectively with
the crucial problem of employment. If they succeed
in this, then it is reasonably certain that educational development in these vast regions will be
smoothly achieved.

Although for the greater part of the adult
peasant population of the developing countries recent scientific and technological progress has not
dispelled the feeling that nowadays it is becoming
more difficult to die, the young generation looks
at things in a very different light. Thanks to the
spread of education and the mass media of information and communication, young people are becoming
increasingly aware, on the one hand, of the enormous potentialities opened up to their countries by
technological progress and, on the other hand, of
governmental incapacity to take full advantage of
this progress and satisfy the young generation's
legitimate aspirations.

In this new world, which is evolving at an unprecedented pace, the young generation has the right
to assert itself and demand its rightful place in
the new social order that is now taking shape.[18]
It should be added that it is the university students who will play the predominant role in the con-
quest of this rightful place. By reason of its numbers and intellectual qualifications, academic youth
can exert great influence in the shaping of a juster
and more human social order during the coming years.
The hundreds of thousands of university students
who will be graduating during the next few decades
will form the intellectual infrastructure of the
countries of the Third World. This is a fact of
life of which those responsible for social and economic progress in their various countries must
never lose sight.

NOTES

1. See The New York Times, January 5, 1969.

2. See E. Denison, The Sources of Economic Growth in the United States (New York: Committee for Economic Development, 1962).

3. The United Nations and other international agencies have published several studies on the role of science and technology in the process of development. Here is a selection of the most important studies on the subject: Politiques et moyens propres à promouvoir le progrès technique (New York: United Nations, 1969); Science and Technology for Development (New York: United Nations, 1970, Sales No. E.70.I.23); Le développement par la Science (Paris: UNESCO, 1969); Science, croissance économique et politique gouvernementale (Paris: OECD, 1963); World Plan of Action for the Application of Science and Technology to Development (Paris: ECOSOC, 1970).

4. See Politiques et moyens propres à promouvoir le progrès technique, op. cit., pp. 1ff.

5. Typical of the old mentality, which tends to delay the industrial application of one of the most revolutionary discoveries, is the reaction by certain members of the old establishment on the morrow of the first atomic explosion. Thus, in an article published in 1947 in the Bulletin of Atomic Scientists, two American engineers voiced concern about the possibility of a too rapid use of atomic energy. They wrote: "We believe that most of the benefits to be derived by our generation from atomic energy could be assured without using them in the nuclear reactors." They proposed the following compromise solution between the American and Soviet stands: "sign an international agreement declaring that no new nuclear reactor on an industrial

scale will be constructed in the world during a certain number of years." See Angelos Angelopoulos, Will the Atom Unite the World? (London: The Bodley Head, 1957), p. 50.

6. See Le Monde, September 6, 1952, and December 4, 1953.

7. See Angelopoulos, op. cit.

8. See Gordon Dean, Report on the Atom (New York: A. A. Knopf, 1953), p. 216.

9. According to a survey by the economic department of McGraw-Hill published under the title Technological Forecasting and Long-Range Planning (New York: McGraw-Hill, 1969).

10. See Bureau International du Travail, Programme mondial de l'emploi (Geneva, 1969), p. 17.

11. See World Economic Survey, 1968, Part I (New York: United Nations, 1969, Sales No. E.69. II.C.6), p. 9.

12. See BIT, op. cit., p. 39.

13. For the whole of Latin America in 1960, about 40 percent of the active labor force was underemployed and almost 27 percent was completely unemployed. See World Economic Survey, 1968, op. cit., p. 10.

14. See BIT, op. cit., p. 52.

15. See Long-Term Policies and Programmes for Youth in National Development (New York: United Nations, 1971, Sales No. S.N.E.70.IV.12).

16. In Africa, the rate of illiteracy is 47 percent for children of 10 to 14 years, 51 percent for the age group of 15 to 19 years, and 64 percent for young persons of 20 to 24 years. See La planification de l'enseignement: études des problèmes et des perspectives (Paris: UNESCO, 1968).

17. See OECD, <u>L'Observateur de l'OCDE</u>, October, 1968.

18. "The modern world reserves for youth," writes René Maheu, Director General of UNESCO, "a place of a new dimension because both of the numerical force of youth and the specific role it can play in the transformations imposed by the objectives of developments." See <u>Courrier, Youth</u> (Paris, 1969).

9

ECONOMIC GROWTH
AND FORECASTS
OF WORLD INCOME
IN THE YEAR 2000

WILL THE TWENTIETH CENTURY BE THE
CENTURY OF THE THIRD WORLD?

In the preceding chapters we have considered
the factors that could accelerate development in
the countries of the Third World. Should active
international cooperation prove realizable, especially as regards development financing, the effect
on growth rates would be so considerable that the
present alarming gap between rich and poor countries would progressively narrow and a trend would
be initiated toward a more equitable distribution
of world income, that is, a distribution more con-
sistent with the human and material requirements of
each country.

This is the sort of future to which the peoples
of the developing countries aspire. They rightly
believe that the industrial revolution of the twentieth century will assist them to attain the status
to which they are entitled. They are well aware
that the already industrialized countries owe their
success largely to technological progress and the
quality of their manpower.

Great Britain owed its economic leadership in the nineteenth century to the fact that it was the first country to exploit the technological advances of the first industrial revolution. France followed in Great Britain's wake with a certain time-lag, and by 1880 Germany had become the third industrial power in Europe. The United States, aided in the initial stage of its industrialization by European capital and technical know-how, was to become the dominant capitalist power of the twentieth century. The mainspring of all this phenomenal industrial growth was the utilization of energy derived from two new sources: electricity and oil. After World War I and the Russian Revolution, the Soviet Union, thanks largely to its intensive exploitation of technical advances, was soon hard on the heels of the Western capitalist countries and ranked second only to the United States as a world economic power by the beginning of the second half of the twentieth century.

The period between 1950 and 1970 was marked by sustained economic growth throughout the world, and particularly in the industrialized countries. West Germany and Japan, defeated and devastated in World War II, accomplished a miracle of economic recovery and expansion. Within the two decades 1950-70, West Germany increased its GNP fivefold, tripled labor productivity in the industrial sector, and eliminated unemployment and underemployment. West Germany had to revalue its currency twice within ten years, thereby setting a record in world monetary history. Today West Germany is the fourth industrial power in the world and the world's wealthiest creditor country.*

----

*In May, 1971, the official gold and foreign exchange reserves (inclusive of SDR) of West Germany totaled $17 billion and exceeded those of the United States ($14.3 billion) by $2.7 billion. Moreover, they were three times larger than the official reserves of the Banque de France, and accounted for almost half the combined reserves of the Common Market member countries.

However, it is Japan that has achieved the
highest and best sustained growth rate in the world.
In the 15 years from 1955 to 1970, Japan multiplied
its GNP by about eight, from $24 billion to $200
billion. During the 1960's, Japan's average annual
economic growth rate was three times higher than
that of the United States. Such rapid and sustained growth took Japan up from sixth place, which
it held between 1960 and 1965, to third place among
the leading industrial powers, after the United
States and the Soviet Union. Japan's per capita
GNP quadrupled during the past decade and, as compared with $1,625 in 1959, is expected to rise to
$3,590 by 1975. Thus, under its current five-year
plan Japan aims at growth rates higher than any
other nation has ever achieved.

The exceptionally rapid growth of Japan and
West Germany since the war is attributable: (1) to
their possession of an abundant and highly efficient labor force whose skills are constantly kept
up to date and improved thanks to a permanent system of vocational training; (2) to the adoption in
all sectors of the latest scientific and technological advances; and (3) to the fact that a very
large part of their most important industrial installations was wiped out during the war and re-
placed after the war by the best modern machinery
and other equipment, thus giving them an immense
competitive advantage over the other industrially
advanced countries, a large proportion of whose un-
devastated industries continued to use out-dated
and relatively inefficient equipment after the war,
greatly to the detriment of their competitiveness.
If to all this is added the fact that the compulsory
disarmament imposed on the defeated countries at
the end of the war relieved them of a vast burden
of military expenditure while that burden continued
to constitute a serious economic handicap for the
victor countries, it is easy to understand the
astounding economic success that Japan and West
Germany have enjoyed since 1945.

Under these circumstances, would it be wise to
ignore or underestimate the potential impact of

today's revolutionary scientific and technological
advances on the Third World? In a previous work,
we predicted that the industrial use of thermonuclear energy would speed up the emergence of the
developing countries on the international scene.[1]
Now that Japan will, within a short time, have become a powerful factor in the industrialization of
developing countries, it is clear that there are
going to be great changes in the geopolitical map
of the world. All the indications are that in the
course of the twenty-first century economic domination of the world might well be assumed by Asia and
Africa, under the leadership of China. In a prophetic mood, shortly before his death, Charles de
Gaulle said to André Malraux: "Only a single generation now separates the West from the Third
World's 'entree en scene.'"[2]

FORECASTS FOR THE YEAR 2000

We were not being pessimistic when, in an earlier reference to the gap between rich and poor nations, we said that it would widen still further if
the present situation were allowed to continue. On
the contrary, we were optimistic that this danger
could be eliminated if new and more appropriate financing procedures were introduced and if the developing countries drew up, and took radical steps
to implement, plans designed to ensure the most effective possible utilization of future financial
aid. There would then be a possibility of attaining higher growth rates and thereby progressively
narrowing the gap.

Higher growth rates are all the more urgent
since, at the present pace, the poorest of the developing nations, which account for half the total
population of the Third World, would take more than
two centuries to reach the present level of Western
Europe. According to projections of GNP in the
year 2000 by Herman Kahn and Anthony Wiener, by
then the gap between rich and poor nations will
have increased by 43 percent compared with the year
1965.[3]

These disturbing forecasts underline how absolutely necessary it is to achieve faster rates of
growth if the poorer nations are ever to become
able to break out of their state of stagnation, and,
consequently, how essential it is to increase the
flow of genuine development assistance if the following minimum annual growth rates are to be attained: 7 percent during the 1970's, 8 percent
during the 1980's, and 8.5 percent during the
1990's.

Such growth targets should not be regarded as
unrealistic for new countries that are firmly re-
solved to extricate themselves as rapidly as possible from the present impasse and possess the necessary material and human resources to do so. In
its development plan for 1970-75, Japan aims at an
average annual growth in per capita GNP of 13.3
percent at current prices and 9.2 percent at constant prices. The People's Republic of China should
be capable of achieving equal success thanks to its
authoritarian and centralized system and its capacity for assimilating the latest scientific and
technological innovations. The achievement of an
average annual growth rate of 10 percent, already
aimed at in China's five-year plans, would be facilitated if its present apparent desire for active
economic cooperation with the Western world were
realized.

The growth rate in our projections would assure developing nations by the year 2000 of a per
capita income 11 times higher than it was in 1970.
In the light of Japan's eightfold increase in national income in only 15 years, this does not appear to be unduly optimistic.

Estimated World Income in the Year 2000

The bases of our estimate of the total that
world income will have reached by the year 2000 are
as follows:

1. For the industrial countries, we use the
OECD projections for the decade 1970-80. The

projected average annual rates of growth are as
follows: United States 4.7 percent, Canada 5.4
percent, Japan 10 percent, and the OECD European
countries 4.8 percent. According to these projections, the overall GDP will increase by 68 percent
between 1970 and 1980. For the two subsequent decades (1980-2000), the above growth rates are low-
ered by 10 percent, except for Japan and Greece,
where the reduction is put at 30 percent and 20
percent, respectively.

The 7 percent average annual growth rate
adopted by us for Japan coincides fairly closely
with the estimates of the Japanese Economic Planning Agency for the four following 5-year periods:
1971-75, 10.6 percent; 1976-80, 10.6 percent, 1981-
85, 8.5 percent; and 1986-2000, 6.0 percent. These
figures work out to an average of 8.9 percent for
the years 1971-2000.

In our calculations, we assume average annual
growth rates of 10 percent per annum for the decade
1971-80 and 7 percent for the two subsequent decades 1981-2000. However, a number of experts in-
sist that Japan can keep up a growth rate of around
10 percent right up to the end of the century. According to Paul Gregory, "The socio-political
forces that brought about the miracle of the 1950's
and 1960's show no sign of exhaustion."[4] Furthermore, in his projections of the growth of Japan's
economy, Herman Kahn assumes a 9.4 percent average
annual rate for the entire period 1971-2000.[5]

2.   For the developing countries, our calculation is based on the above estimate of income for
1970 and the average annual growth rates also estimated above; 1970-80, 7 percent; 1980-90, 8 percent; and 1990-2000, 8.5 percent.

3.   For the communist countries, exclusive of
the People's Republic of China, for the decade
1970-80 we use the growth rates adopted by the Economic Commission for Europe, which differ from

country to country.* For the period 1980-2000, we
assume a 10 percent reduction.

4. In the case of the People's Republic of
China, we start from the 1970 level of GDP estimated by us above, and calculate the projected levels
for the decade 1970-80 by assuming an average annual growth rate of 8 percent, and those for the
two decades 1980-2000 by putting the average rate
at 9 percent per annum. For the other communist
countries in Asia, we assume growth rates of 7 percent for the first decade and 8 percent for the
last two decades. On the basis of the above as-
sumptions we arrive at the figures set out in Table
23 and Figures 8 and 9. The distribution of world
GDP, estimated in Table 23, according to both stage
of development and socioeconomic system of the different regions, yields the percentage shares shown
in Table 24.

A comparison of the projection of GNP for 1970
and 2000 indicates the following significant trends:

1. The contribution of industrialized countries to world GNP will drop from 84.6 percent to
about 70 percent, or by about 15 points. This contrasts with an almost twofold increase in the contribution of developing countries, i.e., from 15.4
percent in 1970 to 30 percent in 2000.

2. The most pronounced fall in percentage
contribution within the group "industrialized countries" will take place in the market economies,

---

*The growth rates by country are as follows:
Bulgaria, 6.5 percent; Czechoslovakia, 4.9 percent;
East Germany, 4.9 percent; Hungary, 5.0 percent;
Poland, 6.1 percent; Roumania, 7.1 percent; and
Soviet Union, 6.1 percent. In the case of Yugo-
slavia, we apply growth rates of 6 percent and 5.4
percent respectively.

TABLE 23

Projection of World GDP, 1970 and 2000
(billions of U.S. dollars)

	1970	Per-centage	2000	Per-centage
Market economies				
Developed countries				
United States	978	31.8	3,520	21.4
Western Europe	723	23.6	2,680	16.3
Canada	76	2.4	330	2.0
Japan	188	6.2	1,890	11.5
Other countries	60	1.9	145	0.8
Total	2,025	65.9	8,565	52.0
Developing countries				
(non-communist world)	335	10.9	3,200	19.5
Total	2,360	76.8	11,775	71.5
Centrally planned economies				
U.S.S.R.	425	13.8	2,240	13.9
Eastern Europe	150	4.9	710	4.3
People's Republic of China	125	4.1	1,585	9.7
Other countries	12	0.4	108	0.6
Total	712	23.2	4,643	28.5
World total	3,072	100	16,418	100

TABLE 24

Distribution of World GDP, 1970 and 2000

	Billions of U.S. Dollars		Percentage	
Region	1970	2000	1970	2000
Industrialized countries				
Market economies	2,025	8,575	65.9	52
Centrally planned	575	2,950	18.7	18
Total	2,600	11,525	84.6	70
Developing countries				
Market economies	335	3,200	10.9	19.5
Centrally planned	137	1,693	4.5	10.5
Total	472	4,893	15.4	30
Grand total	3,072	16,408	100	100

FIGURE 8

Distribution of World GNP, 1970 and 2000
(percentages)

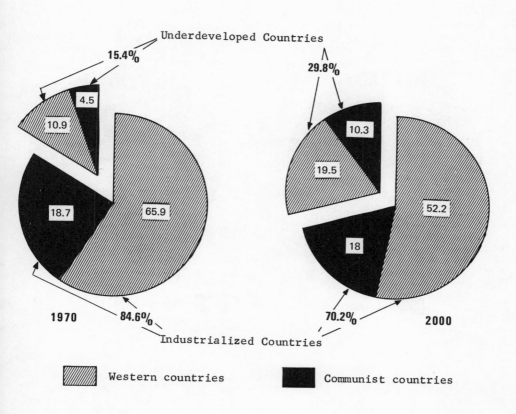

FIGURE 9

Distribution of GNP by Social System, 1970 and 2000

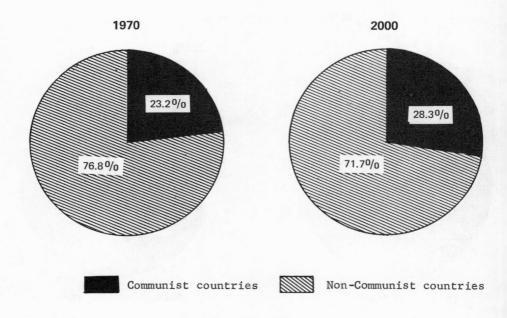

i.e., from 65.9 percent to 52 percent. The percentage contribution of centrally planned countries
in this group will remain virtually unchanged.
Among developing countries, on the other hand,
those with centrally planned economies will more
than double their contribution.

3. In absolute figures, the United States
will retain the lead, although its share of combined world income will drop from 31.8 percent to
21.4 percent or by one-third. Western Europe will
remain second with a 16.3 percent share, while the
Soviet Union and Japan will occupy third and fourth
positions with 13.7 percent and 11.5 percent, respectively.

4. Among the other countries of Asia, the
People's Republic of China will be in the lead in
the year 2000, with a contribution of 9.7 percent.
In that year, the combined share of all the now developing countries in the Third World is expected
to reach nearly 30 percent, as against about 15
percent in 1970. If Japan is included in the calculation, the combined contribution of all the
countries of Asia, Africa, and Latin America will
amount to 41.3 percent in the year 2000, compared
to 22 percent in 1970.

Per Capita Income in 1970 and 2000

The estimates of distribution of world GDP appear in a different light when account is taken of
the divergent growth rates of world population, as
can be clearly seen from the figures in Table 25.

Although the volume of GNP of the Third World
is shown to register a tenfold increase between
1970 and 2000, in terms of GNP per capita the
growth is only fivefold. This trend is attributed
to the fact that population in the developing regions increased twice as fast as in the industrially advanced countries. Meanwhile, the progressive
improvement in living standards of the peoples of
the Third World is expected to reduce the present

TABLE 25

Per Capita GNP by Major Group
of Countries, 1970 and 2000
(U.S. dollars)

Group of Countries	1970	2000
Developed countries (total, including communist countries)	2,330	7,920
Developing countries (total, including communist countries)	190	970
World total	880	2,525

population explosion to normal growth rates before
the end of the century. This, in turn, could bring
about a faster rise in per capita GNP in today's
poor regions of the world.

It is advisable to disaggregate the global
figures of GNP per capita in order to trace probable
trends from 1970 to 1980 and 2000 in selected countries, both capitalist and communist. The estimated changes are shown in Table 26. Although the preceding estimates of GNP by country are based on the
value of the dollar in 1970, in Table 26, which is
exclusively concerned with per capita GNP, we have
taken into account the adjustments resulting from
the international monetary agreement of December,
1971.* It should be noted that all other dollar
estimates in this book are expressed in terms of
1970 dollars.

---

*The resulting percentage changes in exchange
rates against the dollar for several countries were
as follows: France +8.57; Germany +13.58; Italy
+7.48;   Japan +16.88; Sweden +7.49; Switzerland
+13.9;   United Kingdom +8.57.

TABLE 26

Per Capita GNP in Selected Countries, 1970, 1980, 1990, and 2000 (in U.S. dollars at 1972 prices)

Country	1970	1980	1990	2000
United States	4,770	6,600	8,600	11,800
Sweden	4,190	5,700	7,650	10,200
Canada	3,780	5,500	7,600	10,600
Switzerland	3,700	4,700	5,830	7,200
West Germany	3,440	5,200	7,500	10,700
France	3,115	4,900	7,500	11,200
United Kingdom	2,355	3,000	3,600	4,600
Japan	2,220	5,000	9,200	16,500
Italy	1,825	3,000	4,900	7,800
Greece	1,000	1,850	3,200	5,200
Spain	918	1,400	2,160	3,300
Turkey	400	580	850	1,300
Soviet Union	1,775	2,865	--	7,000
Czechoslovakia	1,810	2,760	--	6,000
East Germany	2,070	3,280	--	7,200
Poland	1,200	1,960	--	4,800
Hungary	1,150	1,820	--	4,150
People's Republic of China	165	300	--	1,300
India	105	170	--	550
Brazil	260	380	--	1,000
Mexico	568	850	--	2,200

In terms of per capita GNP, our projections
for the year 2000 reveal a number of changes in the
order of economic importance of industrial countries. Thus, Japan starting ninth in 1970 moves to
fifth place by 1980 and to the top by 1990. Its
progress will accelerate, and in the year 2000 it
will have substantially outdistanced the other
countries. Thus its per capita GNP will be $16,500,
while for the United States, in second place, the
figure will be only $11,800. France will occupy
third place, followed closely by West Germany,
Canada, and Sweden, whose per capita GNP will hover
somewhere around $10,500. The Soviet Union, Switz-
erland, East Germany, and Italy will occupy fourth
rank, with a per capita GNP on the order of $7,000.
The United Kingdom will continue to fall beind.

Japan and the People's Republic of China will
achieve the fastest growth in GNP per capita. Figure 10 shows the evolution of per capita GNP from
1970 to 2000 for selected countries.

Distribution of World Income
by Social System

On the basis of the prevailing political system, irrespective of the stage of economic development, the distribution of world income as between
non-communist and communist countries is shown in
Table 27. In the course of the three decades covered by Table 27, the contribution of the communist
countries is expected to go up from 23.4 percent to
28.3 percent by reason of the fact that their
growth rate is higher than that of the capitalist
countries. The assertion that highly developed
countries cannot maintain a high growth rate for
long does not yet seem to be true of communist
countries which, by reason of their large wealth of
unutilized material resources, may be expected to
maintain high growth rates at least up to the end
of the century. The Soviet Union is planning to
exploit the vast resources of Siberia and to this
end is now actively promoting cooperation with
Western industrial countries. This should enable

FIGURE 10

Per Capita GNP, Selected Countries, 1970 and 2000

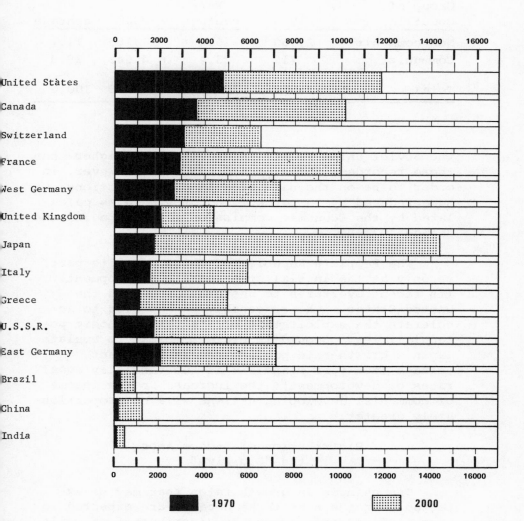

217

TABLE 27

Distribution of World Income by
Country Groups, 1970 and 2000
(billions of U.S. dollars at 1970 prices)

Group of Countries	1970	Per- centage	2000	Per- centage
Non-communist	2,360	76.8	11,765	71.7
Communist	712	23.4	4,643	28.3
Total	3,072	100.0	16,408	100.0

the Soviet Union to attain growth rates higher than
those recorded in the period 1950-70. However, in
order to be on the safe side in our projections, we
have reduced by 10 percent the growth rates calculated by the Economic Commission for Europe for the
decade 1971-80.

The People's Republic of China, for its part,
is only at the initial stage of its development.
Its recent overtures to Western Europe and the
United States might reasonably be expected to accelerate the exploitation of its vast economic potentialities. Should it prove possible to emulate
Japan's growth rate performance (and in fact
China's five-year plans aim at substantially equal
rates of development), the increase in the income
of communist developing nations will be proportion-
ately greater.[6]

Distribution of Income Among
the "Big Five"

The changes in growth rates that may be expected over the next three decades are expected to
have profound effects on the distribution of world
income among the leading economic powers (see Table 28). Thus, it has been estimated that the combined share of the United States and the industrial

TABLE 28

Percentage of World GNP in the
"Big Five," 1970 and 2000

	1970	2000
United States	40.0	29.6
Western Europe	29.7	22.5
Japan	7.7	15.1
Soviet Union	17.5	18.8
People's Republic of China	5.1	14.0
Total	100.0	100.0

countries of Western Europe may decline over the
three decades by some 25 percent and that, while
the position as regards the Soviet Union will remain virtually unchanged, the shares of Japan and
the People's Republic of China will approximately
double and triple, respectively.

By the year 2000, the combined economic
strength of Japan and the People's Republic of
China will be equal to that of the United States.
According to the medium of 9.4 percent average annual growth estimated by Herman Kahn, Japan's GNP
would total $3,000 billion by the year 2000 instead
of the $1,900 billion forecast, and its share of the
combined GNP of the "Big Five" would rise from 15
to 26 percent.[7]

Although Kahn's forecasts seem to us overopti-
mistic, we would agree that Japan will continue to
have an annual growth rate of about 7 percent,
which would be higher than that of the other industrial countries. The expansion of Japan's activity
will be directed primarily toward other Far Eastern
countries, especially the People's Republic of
China. Financial and technical aid extended by
Japan to this region is constantly increasing: between 1966 and 1970, it rose from $625 million to
$1,825 million. Moreover, the United States'

recent change of policy toward the People's Republic of China, together with the present world monetary crisis, will force Japan to look for new commercial outlets. Furthermore, the inherent contradictions of the capitalist system will prove to the advantage of the communist countries by enabling them to accelerate their rate of development. Two major industrial countries, West Germany and Japan, are in fact establishing closer economic links with the Soviet Union and the People's Republic of China, while the United States and other Western countries are preparing to do likewise. Therefore, one can foresee far-reaching changes in the world economic scene in the course of the next decade or so.

IMPACT OF PROJECTED CHANGES ON THE
ROLE OF THE THIRD WORLD

Are the projections we have made reliable? Not everybody will agree with all of them, but we maintain that, on the basis of past experience and the most likely future developments, our forecasts are fairly cautious and reliable.

The realization of our estimates will largely depend on the degree of inflation affecting each country over the next three decades. If inflationary pressures are not allowed to go beyond their present level, there are good grounds for believing that the countries considered here will attain their economic targets. Countries that can succeed in actually lowering present levels of inflation will, by the year 2000, have exceeded the per capita income that we forecast. On the other hand, in countries that are unable to prevent inflation from rising above present levels, income will be lower than predicted.

Should the basic conditions that we have postulated above be fulfilled, the living standards in developing countries would appreciably improve. This would mark the opening of a new phase in which the present ever-widening gap between the rich

and the poor countries would begin to narrow.
Whereas in 1970 per capita income in the industrialized countries was 12 times higher than in the developing countries, by the year 2000 it should be
only eight times higher. Therefore, instead of
continuing to increase, as in the past, the income
disparity will have lessened by one-third.

Thus, at the end of the century the countries
of Asia, Africa, and Latin America would be on the
way to transforming themselves into a powerful economic and political group of nations destined to
play a decisive role on the world stage during the
twenty-first century. Europe and North America,
which together produced 78 percent of world income
in 1970, would account for only 57 percent in 2000
and only 44 percent by the year 2025. The remaining 56 percent would then be coming from the countries of Asia (including Japan), Africa, and Latin
America, which at present produce only 15 percent.
Thus, the world would gradually arrive at a distribution of its wealth more in proportion to the
regional distribution of its population.

Would this evolution constitute a challenge by
the Third World to the industrialized countries
that at present dominate the world market and the
world political scene?[8] The ultimate consequences
of such a challenge, arising from the social and
economic progress of the Third World, will be determined by the manner in which today's rich countries decide to meet it.

NOTES

1. See Angelos Angelopoulos, <u>Will the Atom Unite the World</u>? (London: The Bodley Head, 1957), p. 181.

2. See André Malraux, <u>Les chênes qu'on abat</u> (Paris: Gallimard, 1971), p. 98.

3. GDP (in billions of U.S. dollars at 1965 prices):

Developing countries	1965	2000
Africa	43.5	216.0
Asia (exclusive of Japan)	203.4	1,081.0
South America	59.8	292.0
Total	306.7	1,589.0
Developed countries		
Japan	84.0	1,056.0
North America	774.2	3,620.0
Oceania	28.0	107.0
Europe	923.9	4,476.0
Total	1,810.1	9,259.0
World total	2,116.8	10,848.0

Per Capita GDP (in U.S. dollars at 1965 prices):

	1965	2000
Developing countries	135	325
Developed countries	1,675	5,775
World total	631	1,696

<u>Source</u>: Herman Kahn and Anthony Wiener, <u>Toward the Year 2018</u> (New York: Foreign Policy Association, 1968), p. 157.

4. See "Le modèle japonais: perspectives d'avenir," in <u>Futuribles</u>, July-August, 1971, p. 900.

5. See Herman Kahn, <u>The Emerging Japanese Superstate</u> (London: Deautsch, 1971), p. 127.

6. See R. Guillan, <u>Dans 30 ans la Chine</u> (Paris: Seuil, 1965). In a seminar on international economic questions held at Davos, Switzerland,

in January, 1971, one of the experts on Asian issues, Tibor Mende, emphasized that "Japan is an
example to follow for the developing countries."

7.   See Kahn, op. cit., p. 128.   On the role
of Japan in tomorrow's world, see also: Hakan
Hedberg, Le défi japonais (Paris: Denoël), 1970);
P. Quillain, Le Japon (Paris: Seuil, 1967); Saburo
Okita and Y. Hanayana, The Japanese Economy and
Economic Development in Asia 1900-2000 (Tokyo,
1970).

8.   "For societies just as for individuals,"
writes Jean-Jacques Servan-Schreiber, "there is no
growth without challenge. Progress is a battle as
life is a fight."   See Jean-Jacques Servan-Schreiber,
Le défi américain (Paris: Denoël, 1967), p. 335.

10

WILL CHINA
BECOME
THE SPOKESMAN
FOR THE
THIRD WORLD?

THE SIGNIFICANCE OF CHINA'S ENTRY
INTO THE UNITED NATIONS

It is certain that in the years that lie ahead the position of the developing countries will be greatly strengthened by the recent entry of the People's Republic of China into the forum of the United Nations.

The decision of the General Assembly on October 25, 1971, to give the People's Republic of China full rights and prerogatives in that international organization, and consequently in all the specialized institutions associated with it, confers on China a status that will enable it to derive great advantages in several different domains.

International Significance

First, in the international domain China, by its activities in the UN will henceforth be able to prove itself a defender of the spirit of the Charter and a promoter of radical structural reforms within the UN. All the indications are that, despite its previous hostility, China will respect the principles embodied in the Charter. According to the

explanatory memorandum submitted in support of the
Albanian motion, whose text was without doubt approved beforehand by Peking, the entry of China
into the UN "is more than ever a matter of vital importance, particularly for the future of that or-
ganisation" and "the People's Republic of China has
always shown complete respect for the independence
and dignity of other states."[1]

Furthermore, China will press for important
changes in the structure of this world institution,
and this at a time when the latter is passing
through a critical period in its history. "The
United Nations," said Chou En-lai on June 24, 1967,
"must be completely reorganized and transformed;
they must abandon their power policy, and there
must be equality for all countries, large or small."
China's main desire at the moment is to see an end
put to the game at present being played by the two
most powerful members of the UN, the United States
and the Soviet Union, and the creation of a new
equilibrium. Henceforth, the struggle for the lead
will not be bipolar but tripolar, and each of the
three poles will attract the largest possible number
of adherents. So far as the Third World countries
are concerned, they will seek to benefit by this
rivalry among the economic and political giants, a
rivalry that will accelerate technological progress
to the benefit of the whole of humanity.

It is to be hoped that, thanks to this new
equilibrium, the UN will at last lose its ineffectualness vis-à-vis the great problems of the day.
In future efforts to arrive at an equitable settlement of the world's major problems, it seems probable that the Third World countries will look to
the People's Republic of China to support their
aspirations.

Economic Significance

Second, in the economic sphere, the People's
Republic of China, having become a member of the
international community, will take advantage of

this fact to extend its business relations with all
countries of the world, and particularly the great
industrialized countries, thereby accelerating its
own development to a degree far beyond even the
most optimistic forecasts.

All the developed countries are at present preparing to broaden their business relations with
China and, in the competition to conquer this vast
Asiatic market, Japan, with its well-known dynamism,
will be an important factor in the acceleration of
the development of all Asiatic countries and particularly mainland China. To form some idea of the
great possibilities for Japanese trade with that
country, one has only to note that, whereas Japan's
exports to Formosa in 1969 amounted to $606 million,
the value of its exports to mainland China, with a
population 50 times larger, was only $390 million.

It should not be forgotten that if one day
Formosa is reunited with the People's Republic of
China, it will be able to make an extremely valuable contribution to the progress of the Chinese
territories as a whole since this island is a highly industrialized region and has a competent labor
force that would be an invaluable factor in the
modernization of the Chinese economy, in the rapid
assimilation of modern technology by the mainland
regions, and in the adoption of new methods of management.

Thus, the reputation of the People's Republic
of China as a great economic power will be established, first in the countries of the Third World,
and then throughout the whole of the international
market.

Ideological and Political Significance

Third, in the ideological and political domain
there can be no doubt that China's activities in
the UN and in the international scene, in addition
to the acceleration of its economic growth, will
favorably affect its ideological and political

influence, particularly among the developing countries.

China's success in transforming its economic
and social structure smoothly and peacefully, with
the cooperation of the existing bourgeois cadres
(particularly those concerned with entrepreneurial
administration and management) contrasts favorably
with the results achieved by the procedures adopted
in other communist countries.

Those developing countries that are seeking
desperately to improve their living standard might
be tempted to follow China's example. The mere
presence of China at the UN, and its abstention
from any interference in the internal affairs of
other countries, will strengthen the revolutionary
movements and galvanize the dynamic elements in the
Third World countries which, inspired by the Chinese
doctrine, may seek to restructure their economic and
political system even by recourse to violent action.

THE IMPORTANCE OF A RESUMPTION OF
CHINA'S ECONOMIC RELATIONS
WITH THE OUTSIDE WORLD

For a long time mainland China has been seeking to end its economic and political isolation.
Conscious of its requirements, and of the necessity
to obtain from abroad, in ever-increasing quantity,
the equipment indispensable for speeding up its industrial development, the People's Republic of
China has been endeavoring to open up its frontiers
as rapidly as possible so as to make its market ac-
cessible to foreign, and in particular American,
producers.

During a visit to Peking in September, 1956, as
a member of a Greek delegation that was representa-
tive of a variety of ideological tendencies, in the
course of a conversation with Chinese Prime Minister Chou En-lai, I asked whether China would be dis-
posed to begin talks with the countries of the West

with a view to the resumption of commercial relations with them, and in particular with the United
States, on the basis of long-term trade agreements.
Pointing out that the United States, which at that
time had a military budget of about $35 billion,
would experience difficulty in getting its economy
back onto an even keel, I tried to discover whether
China could assure the United States of a succession of large orders over a long period, a development that would help to bring about an international
détente and create the conditions indispensable for
active and constructive coexistence. Here is Chou
En-lai's reply, as set out in a book of mine published in Greece in January, 1957. The views he
then expressed remain entirely valid in the conditions that prevail today:

> There you touch on a fundamental prob-
> lem. You are right, and the idea is
> sound. Arms production increases in-
> ternational tension. Military expendi-
> ture places a heavy burden on all peo-
> ples, ourselves included; it is an ob-
> stacle to the improvement of the stan-
> dard of living. Unquestionably, if
> long-term commercial cooperation were
> possible between East and West, this
> would be to the great benefit of the
> whole world.
>   Is this possible? China is ready
> to do all in her power to make it so.
> As to your question about a long-term
> trade agreement with the United States,
> China is equally ready to take part in
> discussions with a view to the conclu-
> sion of such an agreement. We need
> machinery and other capital goods
> that America produces. We know that
> American industry is highly developed,
> and we admire the quality of its prod-
> ucts. But we also need to increase
> our own exports. What then is the
> policy we should adopt? Don't forget
> that it is the United States that has

imposed an embargo on us and keeps us
in a state of isolation. [2]

These remarks were made at the time when China
was on the eve of its rupture with the Soviet Union
and was endeavoring to reduce its economic dependence on that country by entering into trade relations with other countries. However, the United
States, persisting in its short-sighted policy, refused to consider any suggestions of this nature.

It is certain that if, since that time, the
United States had resumed economic relations with
the People's Republic of China, China's economic
growth would have been accelerated and its GNP
would have risen above the present per capita level
of $165. Although such developments might not have
brought about any appreciable change in the international economic situation, the political climate
created by close collaboration between the two countries would have had favorable repercussions on the
international plane in general. And, looking back
to a still earlier period, if the United Nations had
agreed to the demand presented to it on November 18,
1949, by Chou En-lai, then Minister for Foreign Affairs, and had recognized the government of the
People's Republic of China as the sole government
of the entire Chinese people, it is possible that
the war in Korea, and subsequently that in Vietnam,
might not have grown to such proportions and lasted
so long or, indeed, might have been avoided altogether. It must not be forgotten that the embargo
imposed on China not only slowed down its development but, directly or indirectly, helped to poison
international relations in that part of the world
by prolonging deadly conflicts there.

When one thinks of the enormous human and material losses suffered by all the countries involved in these still unresolved conflicts, and
when one considers how the present international
situation continues to be bedeviled by them, one
can only wonder by what aberration the world's responsible authorities have failed to adopt a less

rigid policy that would have saved the world so
much misery and so many useless sacrifices. Must
we conclude, to quote Gaston Bouthoul, that "the
phenomenon of war" is a "geopolitical fatality"?
We do not believe that his is so, and Mr. Bouthoul
himself emphasizes that "if one desires peace, one
must know what war means," that is to say, study
its nature, causes and functions, and the rhythmic
or cyclical nature of its occurrence.[3]

TOWARD CONSTRUCTIVE INTERNATIONAL COOPERATION

The course of events over the two decades
1950-70 shows how disastrous a situation can be
brought about by a narrow and short-sighted policy
that, in the end, profits nobody, least of all
those by whom it was conceived.

As regards the future, it is above all China
that will benefit by the widening of its commercial
relations with the large industrial countries,
whereas the United States, which will hereafter participate in this cooperation, will no longer be the
privileged party as would have been the case if the
cooperation had begun fifteen years ago.

Taking into consideration China's enormous
human and material potential, the immensity of its
as yet unexploited resources, its ability to assimi-
late new advances in science and technology, its to-
talitarian system which facilitates the attainment of
full employment, and the growing inflow of foreign
capital, it would seem reasonable to anticipate an
economic growth rate in China similar to that
achieved in Japan in the course of the last twenty
years. If China were in fact to succeed in equal-
ing Japan's performance as regards economic growth
rates, its national income would exceed the figure
we arrived at in our estimates in Chapter 9.

If, in fact, during the years 1970-2000 China,
as was the case for Japan in 1950-70, attained a
growth rate of 11 percent (which is not far from

the 10 percent aimed at in China's present five-
year plan), its share in world income in the year
2000 would be 15.2 percent, instead of 9.7 percent
as estimated by us. If the comparison were limited
to the "Big Five," this would show a higher share
by China in the GNP of this group of countries (see
Table 29).

TABLE 29

Percentage of World GNP in the "Big Five,"
1970 and 2000 (Revised)

	1970	2000 (a)	2000 (b)	Per Capita GNP (in dollars)
United States	40	29.6	27.3	11,800
Western Europe	20.7	22.5	20.7	7,300
Japan	7.7	15.1	14	13,600
Soviet Union	17.5	18.8	17.4	7,000
People's Republic of China	5.1	14	20.6	2,280

[a]According to our prudent estimates.

[b]Assuming a growth rate of 11 percent for China.

Given favorable conditions, China might well
produce one-fifth of the total income of the "Big
Five" group in the year 2000. In that case, China
would be producing an income roughly equal to that
of Western Europe, and higher than that of the Soviet Union and Japan. Nevertheless, its per capita
GNP, amounting to about $2,280, would be far behind
that of the other four countries in the group (see
Table 29). If, however, we look a further 25 years
ahead to the year 2025, even if China's economic

growth rate fell somewhat below 11 percent--perhaps
to 8.5 percent--China would still outstrip the rest
of the "Big Five." In terms of volume, China would
account for 40 percent of the "Big Five" total (as
against 5 percent at present), and for about twice
as much as the United States. However, China's per
capita income would still be only half that of the
United States. In China, per capita earnings would
be only $11,000, as against $23,000 in the United
States.

It should be added that the People's Republic
of China will not be the only country to benefit by
this evolution. The other developing countries, and
indeed the developed countries as well, will necessarily be associated with this new economic circuit.
The admission of China to the UN, the resumption of
diplomatic and economic relations between the United
States and China, the negotiation of Great Britain's
entry into the Common Market, the reorientation of
Soviet policy toward more active cooperation with
the West, the détente that is becoming more apparent
throughout the world--all these important features
of 1971 prove that the new era now opening brings
the prospect of a better future for the whole of
humanity.

NOTES

1. See the article of Alain Bouc in Le Monde,
October 28, 1971, which reprints extracts of this
memorandum and supports the thesis of China's loy-
alty to the United Nations, stating that the People's Republic of China "is neither the Trojan horse
nor the wolf in the sheepfold" but "the messenger of
the last chance."

2. Angelos Angelopoulos, The New China, in
Greek (Athens: Sideris, 1957), p. 135.

3. Gaston Bouthoul, Traité de Polémologie,
Sociologie des guerres (Paris: Payot, 1970). One
should also note the publications of Bouthoul's

Institut de Polémologie, as well as the classic
work of Raymond Aron, <u>Paix et Guerre entre les
Nations</u> (Paris: Calmann-Levy), and the very interesting study by Umberto Campagnola, <u>La paix--une
idée révolutionnaire</u>, a special edition of the
journal <u>Comprendre</u> (Venice), 1968.

Having read the foregoing pages, the reader
might naturally ask the following questions: Although the drastic reforms here proposed for dealing with the problems of social and economic development may be based on irrefutable facts, and their
logic may be unassailable, could they actually be
put into practice? If so, how soon, and what are
their chances of success?

The author has repeatedly stressed that the
present difficulties must not be underestimated.
He is convinced that a precondition for any effective solution is that all those directly concerned
should fully realize the magnitude of the dangers
inherent in the division of the world into privileged and unprivileged nations.

However, that is not enough. The success of
the proposed financing plan will depend not only
on how far the rich industrial countries realize
the seriousness of the problem of underdevelopment
but also on the manner in which they accept and
fulfill their responsibilities toward the poor nations.

At the same time, one is forced to wonder
whether the rich countries are fully conscious of

their duties to one another: Are they acting for motives of enlightened self-interest? One is reminded
of the pressing issue that "Man has succeeded in sub-
duing the atom; will he know how to control his self-
ishness?"--to quote the words of Pope Paul VI. Have
the rich countries realized what risks they will be
called to face in the not far distant future if, despite the multiplying danger signals, they persist
in remaining isolated in their exclusive club of af-
fluence or fool's paradise? Is it necessary to re-
mind people of the admonition given before his death
by the eminent atomic physicist J. Robert Oppen-
heimer: "When vast populations, living today on the
threshold of starvation and misery, become aware of
their condition and ours, it is then that I fear
about what may happen."

Can one ignore the emergence of the Third World
on the international scene, which is bound to be
hastened by the implacable process of far-reaching
transformation of social, economic, and political
structures? Is it wise to lose sight of the fact
that before the end of the century the Third World,
inclusive of the People's Republic of China, will
possess a labor force totaling 3.5 billion persons,
as against a mere 600 million in the industrial countries? Are the leaders of the developed countries
not yet awake to the fact that the world's balance
of economic and political power will be upset when
these huge manpower reserves have had the benefit
of universal education and vocational training and
have at their disposal all the scientific and technological advances, present and future?

A conflict between rich and poor nations will
become inevitable sooner or later unless it can be
prevented by a concerted and realistic policy inspired by international solidarity and the principle
of the indivisibility of prosperity. If mankind is
a community of peoples, then rich nations should extend their social and economic policies beyond their
own frontiers and finance their application to poor
nations as they do domestically in support of low-
income sections of the population. Such a new approach to the problem of socioeconomic development

would benefit the entire world and, in particular,
the industrial countries themselves. A policy of enlightened self-interest as advocated herein would
progressively narrow the immense gap separating rich
and poor nations. Moreover, by creating a climate
of mutual understanding it would promote active cooperation within a better and more humane world.

While the responsibility of industrial countries is indisputable, developing nations too have
an immense stake in the success of concerted efforts
to improve their lot. They have been entrusted with
imperative duties to their own peoples and to the
world community of nations. They are called upon to
adopt, without delay, effective policy measures to
mobilize their material and human resources and
thereby satisfy the aspirations of their peoples for
a better standard of living and greater opportunities for cultural and spiritual advancement.

Within the international framework of concerted action, the role of the United Nations is crucial. After abandoning its passive attitude and
adapting its activities to changing conditions, the
United Nations should become the enlightened guide
of peoples in their struggle for progress and welfare.

The realization of the proposed reforms, as
outlined in this work, such as the reorganization
of the World bank to enable it to operate as the
specialized agency for the financing of developing
countries, the alleviation of the developing countries' burden of outstanding debt, and the free
transfer to them of a percentage of the GNP of the
rich countries--all these far-reaching changes fall
within the purposes of the United Nations. This is
equally true as regards the sharing of the gain
from an eventual upward revaluation of gold.

The future will show whether the industrialized
countries, the developing countries, and the United
Nations will prove farsighted enough to act in a concerted manner and coordinate their efforts so as to
assure world prosperity and preserve world peace.

APPENDIX: CALCULATION OF THE 1970 GNP OF COMMUNIST COUNTRIES

As stated in Chapter 6 of this study, an attempt will be made to estimate the GNP of the communist countries according to Western methods of computation.

SOME CLARIFICATIONS ON THE CONCEPT OF NATIONAL INCOME

In order to avoid possible confusions it would be useful at first to clarify the different concepts of national income according to Western methods of calculation.

First, it is essential to distinguish between gross domestic product (GDP), gross national product (GNP), and national income.

Gross domestic product (GDP) at market prices, the most useful aggregate in terms of economic planning, measures the value of all the goods and services produced within a specified period (a year) by all factors of production resident in the territory of a given country, irrespective of ownership. In other words, GDP includes the earnings of foreign-owned factors of production.

Gross national product (GNP) at market prices equals GDP minus net income payments abroad. In the developed countries, the statistical discrepancy between GDP and GNP is insignificant. By contrast, in the developing nations this discrepancy between the two totals is more significant since net payments abroad for foreign investments often are substantial.

In the subsequent projections, the two concepts are considered as identical. If from gross product (domestic or national) we subtract depreciation charges equal to the consumption of durable capital goods (machinery and other fixed installations), we obtain the net national product (NNP). When from net national product we deduct further indirect taxes levied by the central government and public authorities, less subsidy payments, we arrive at the figure of national income at factor cost. Thus, national income equals disposable income distributed among the factors of production of goods and services (in the form of salaries, wages, profits, rent, etc.). In relation to gross national product, national income is inferior by 20-25 percent.

Although net output is both an appropriate and useful measure of the volume of goods and services devoted to consumption and investment, it raises several practical difficulties that prevent its use as an adequate aggregate in international comparisons. One of the difficulties is associated with the calculation of depreciation charges, which is often arbitrary. National income at factor cost is furthermore affected by changes in fiscal legislation concerning such matters as indirect taxes and subsidy payments. Thus international comparisons are based on gross data.

NET MATERIAL PRODUCT ACCORDING TO THE SOVIET CONCEPT

According to Soviet sources, national income, which equals the "material production of the country," is defined as "the newly created value in productive goods and services." Economic activities considered "productive" are agriculture, industry, construction, transport and communications, wholesale and retail trade, and repairs. This concept does not include economic activities that do not contribute directly to material production, such as the so-called nonmaterial services, i.e., public administration and national defense, personal services, and other such activities. Thus, the term net material product (NMP) applies to communist countries and gross national product (GNP) to Western or market economy countries. The difficulties encountered in arriving at an estimate of GNP per capita for countries with different socioeconomic systems stem from these conceptual differences.

Consequently, the main problem consists in finding a coefficient of conversion assuring the indispensable degree of consistency for comparisons of national income data computed according to different methods. In order to make the aggregate of NMP commensurate to GNP, the NMP must be increased by the value of the sector of nonmaterial services, included in the gross product according to the Western method of national accounts, and by the amount of "depreciation" charges since the material product is computed "net" and not "gross."

CONVERSION BETWEEN SOVIET AND WESTERN MODELS

What coefficient of conversion from one national account model to another should we adopt? It is here that we encounter the greatest difficulties. In order to deal with this crucial problem and eliminate the existing gap, we resorted to the Directorate General of the Statistical Service of the Soviet Union. Its reply of November 6, 1970, drew our attention to the estimates as computed by its own service in order to compare the two sets of national income data. In fact, for making comparisons of East and West national income figures, the Statistical Service of the Soviet Union applied "the method in force in the U.S.S.R. without taking into account incomes generated in the nonproductive sectors of material goods."

This estimate, published for the first time in the Statistical Yearbook of the National Economy of the U.S.S.R. for the Year 1968 (p. 146), provides statistical data for both global and per capita national income for Western countries and the Soviet Union. According to these figures, the national income of ten Western countries, when computed by the Soviet method, is inferior by the average of 29 percent compared to national income calculated according to the Western method of estimation. Consequently, to convert into Western national income data the value computed according to the Soviet method, an increase of 39.5 percent is necessary.[1]

This coefficient of conversion could have been accepted as valid provided both the economic structure of communist countries were almost similar to that of Western industrialized market economies and the method of estimation of national produce--exclusive of services--were identical. However, this identity does not exist. The share of the "service" sector, particularly in Eastern Europe, is inferior compared to Western countries, whereas the "material product" figures published by the communist countries do not include depreciation charges.

In order to arrive at an alignment of the two methods of national income estimation, we have adopted the following procedures:

1. We have calculated estimated contribution of services in the GNP of the communist countries on the basis of the figures published by the Economic Commission for Europe for the year 1963.[2] These have been adjusted for the year 1970. The value of the services of national defense also have been added. The percentage contribution of the "service" sector varies from 14 percent to 23 percent.[3]

2. We have estimated the depreciation charges (by branch of economic activity).

3. We have applied exchange rates published by the Statistical Commission of the United Nations.[4]

According to our calculations, the 1970 GNP by country is shown in Table A-1.

This calculation of GNP of Eastern block countries according to Western methods of national accounts gives an idea of the global income of this entire group in U.S. dollars and per capita. The Soviet Union accounts for the largest share of the combined GNP of communist countries, namely 75.6 percent as against 24.4 percent for Eastern Europe. By contrast, in terms of GNP per capita, Eastern Germany ranks first with $2,068, followed by Czechoslovakia with $1,810, whereas the Soviet Union occupies a close third place with a per capita GNP of $1,756.

APPENDIX TABLE 1

GNP of Communist Countries, 1970

Country	GNP (millions of U.S. dollars)	Per Capita GNP (U.S. dollars)
Bulgaria	7,824	924
Czechoslovakia	26,145	1,810
Eastern Germany	35,311	2,068
Hungary	11,830	1,147
Poland	39,173	1,199
Roumania	16,668	833
Soviet Union	424,425	1,756
Total	561,376	

ESTIMATION OF GNP OF THE PEOPLE'S REPUBLIC OF CHINA

Certain clarifications are in order concerning the method of calculation of the GNP of the People's Republic of China. In the World Bank Atlas 1970, the World Bank, by applying the Soviet method, has arrived at a GNP per capita of $90 in 1968 and accepts an average annual growth rate of 0.3 percent for the period of 1961-68.

However, a number of Western and Chinese sources support our view that the World Bank figures, both as regards the volume of GNP and the average annual rate of growth, are rather unrealistic. According to estimates by Zimmerman, Eckstein, and Hollister for the period 1952-55, the GNP per capita ranged from $80 to $145. Paul Bairoch, who carried out all these calculations, puts the GNP per capita at about $70 in 1953.[5] Moreover, the same author concludes that the average annual rate of economic growth for the period 1957-65 approached 6 percent, while the GDP rose from $100 in 1958 to $130 in 1965.

With all these estimates in mind, we are inclined to believe that the 1960 GNP per capita of
the People's Republic of China exceeded the $88 fig-
ure accepted by the World Bank and that, although
the cultural revolution had undoubtedly slowed down
the country's economic development, nevertheless
the average annual growth during the 1960's must
have been significantly higher than the 0.3 percent
rate accepted by the World Bank.

Moreover, the Chinese press claimed in January, 1971, that "the third five-year plan (1966-70)
was successfully fulfilled" and that "agriculture
has achieved good harvests during this period."[6]
Furthermore, according to Japan's Planning Agency,
the GNP of the People's Republic of China rose 10
percent in 1970.

For all the aforesaid reasons, we believe that
tne NMP per capita in 1970 must have greatly exceeded the World Bank estimates. This assertion is
corroborated by figures given in February, 1971, by
Premier Chou En-lai in an interview to Edgar Snow.
According to the Premier of the People's Republic
of China, in 1970 the value of industrial production totaled $90 billion and that of agriculture
$30 billion. Thus, the aggregate value of these
two sectors reached $120 billion, exclusive of the
value of the sectors of transport and services.[7]

The figures mentioned by Premier Chou En-lai
can only provide indirect support to an independent
parallel estimate of China's gross material product
(GMP) since they do not include the value of transport and the service sector and, moreover, they
refer to "gross" and not to "net" material product.
As is well known, "gross" product differs from
"net" product by including the value of internal
inputs among different enterprises and other in-
termediate transactions, as well as all other purchases from other domestic sectors and through
imports. Consequently, it would be wrong to assert, as proposed by some experts, that the volume
of gross output can be equated to "national income."

However, the figures of industrial and agricultural production can assist in our attempt to arrive at a more approximate empirical estimate of the real magnitude. By applying both the Soviet ratios of gross net output, which should be approximately the same for the People's Republic of China (in the case of China we apply a ratio of 50 percent for industry and 80 percent for agriculture), and the relation between the product of these sectors and the total net material product (this relation is 73 percent in the Soviet Union), we estimate the NNP of China for 1970 at $95 billion. After increasing this NNP by some 30 percent--instead of 35 percent in the case of the Soviet Union--as the estimated value of the service sector and depreciation charges, we arrive at a global GNP on the order of $125 billion and a per capita GNP of $165 (according to the Statistical Commission of the United Nations, the population of mainland China is estimated at 760 million in 1970).

NOTES

1. National income per capita in 1968 (U.S. dollars at 1964 prices), calculated according to the Soviet and Western methods for a number of Western countries and the Soviet Union is shown below:

	Soviet Method	Western Method
United States	2,522	3,544
Soviet Union	1,136	n.a.
Switzerland	1,686	2,248
Sweden	1,655	2,300
Canada	1,504	2,211
Austria	1,385	1,822
West Germany	1,289	1,666
France	1,249	1,758
United Kingdom	1,170	1,670
Netherlands	1,144	1,589
Belgium	1,104	1,699
	14,708	20,518

Soviet figures are inferior in relation to Western method by 28.3 percent. Western figures are superior in relation to Soviet method by 39.5 percent.

2. See Economic Survey for Europe, Part I
(Geneva: United Nations, 1970), p. 7.

3. The estimated share of the "service" sector in net output and the U.S. dollar's exchange
rate are shown by country below.

Country	Nonmaterial Ser- vices Including National Defense	U.S. $ Exchange Rate Used for Conversion
Eastern Germany	22.5	4.20
Bulgaria	16.8	1.60
Roumania	14.2	15.00
Hungary	19.6	30.00
Poland	15.5	24.00
Czechoslovakia	22.6	15.28
Soviet Union	23.2	0.90

4. See United Nations, Monthly Bulletin of
Statistics, December, 1970, p. 202.

5. See Paul Bairoch, Diagnostic de l'évolu-
tion économique du tiers-monde 1900-1968 (Paris:
Gauthier-Villars, 1970), p. 201.

6. See Le Monde, January 9, 1971. The average annual growth rates fixed by the third five-
year plan (1966-70) were 4.4 percent for agriculture and 12 percent for industry. These growth
targets do seem to have been partly realized. According to certain sources in Hong Kong, during the
third five-year plan agriculture achieved a 2-3
percent growth and industry an expansion of 5-7
percent. See Jan Deleyne, L'économie chinoise
(Paris: Seuil, 1971), p. 30.

7. This interview was published in the Ital-
ian review Epoca and was reproduced in outline by
the international press, and in particular by Le
Monde, March 2, 1971, and The Economist, March 13,
1971, which found these figures highly reliable.

ANGELOS ANGELOPOULOS, formerly professor at
the University of Athens, is an economist known
both in Greece and internationally for his scientific activities and his numerous works on economic
and social questions. For a number of years he was
Director of the Economic Council of Greece, and
later he founded and presided over the Greek Economic Planning Association, which formulated the
bases for Greece's first five-year plan.

Professor Angelopoulos is a member of a number
of international institutes concerned with political economy, public finance, statistics, and demographic questions. He is a frequent contributor to
several leading journals and newspapers and lectures at various universities.

Among his more recent publications are <u>Planisme
et Progrès Social</u>, <u>Will the Atom Unite the World?</u>
(this book, in which he examines the economic aspects of atomic energy, has been translated into
12 languages), and <u>Theory and Policy of Economic
Development</u> (in Greek).

In 1967 Professor Angelopoulos resigned from
his post as Rector of the Panteios School of Political Sciences in Athens and since then has lived in
Geneva. He studied economics in Greece, Germany,
and France.